"A personal history which reveals the trials and eventual triumph of the human spirit. A profoundly moving reflection on life's journey, recounted with a remarkable blend of pathos and humor."

–G.B. Gurland, Author

"My Father Called Me Bobby takes a poignant look at family, friends, and relationships, moving from the conservative 50s to the hippie 60s to the hedonistic 70s and beyond. Robert Scherma explores faith, sexuality, love and loss with grace and humor."

–Kate Walter, Author of *Looking for a Kiss: A Chronicle of Downtown Heartbreak and Healing*

"Bob Scherma's book is a charming, funny and ultimately tragic evocation of growing up in Brooklyn in the 1950s and 60s with a zany Italian family and confronting the different aspects of his nature: spirituality versus gay sexuality. Scherma's buoyant spirit, wit, passion for helping people and love for his family and his life partner make this book a joy to read. It is also an inspirational journey, as a portrayal of a man struggling with many losses who eventually turns to his spiritual nature to make a meaningful life despite crushing grief."

–Erica Manfred, Author of *He's History, You're Not & Surviving Divorce After Forty.*

"As I read 'Bobby,' the characters all came to life for me as I grew up with all of them. The faces, the voices, the laughter, and the screaming. It was a Brooklyn Italian Family in full glory. But as I dug deeper, I started to understand the journey Bob went on and continues to do so in his life. The search for how a young Italian man in the 1950s figuring out who he really was the journey of a lifetime. Following his story gave me so much insight into who he was and who he was becoming. I was there for much of it but not until I read this book did I truly understand what that journey truly was. Hopefully it will be a journey that many will understand and hopefully garner some insight into themselves."

–Frank Scherma, President, *Radical Media*; Chairman and CEO of *The Television Academy*

Robert F. Scherma studied psychology at Yeshiva University and the Karen Horney Institute for Psychodynamic Psychotherapy in New York City. He practices psychotherapy with adults in Manhattan's Greenwich Village. He worked in Brooklyn and the Bronx public high schools as a teacher, counselor, and psychologist and considers himself lucky to have loved his chosen professions. He's been spiritual since childhood and remains so to this very day. He experienced love in several forms and suffered many losses of those he loved. Despite those losses, he still feels that life is worth living, especially if there's more fun to be had.

FOR BERYL

Robert F. Scherma

My Father Called Me Bobby

AUSTIN MACAULEY PUBLISHERS™

LONDON * CAMBRIDGE * NEW YORK * SHARJAH

Ordering Information
Quantity sales: Special discounts are available on quantity purchases by corporations, associations, and others. For details, contact the publisher at the address below.

Publisher's Cataloging-in-Publication data
Scherma, Robert F.
My Father Called Me Bobby

ISBN 9781647505356 (Paperback)
ISBN 9781647505363 (Hardback)
ISBN 9781647505417 (ePub e-book)

Library of Congress Control Number: 2021909409

www.austinmacauley.com/us

First Published (2021)
Austin Macauley Publishers LLC
40 Wall Street, 33rd Floor, Suite 3302
New York, NY 10005
USA

mail-usa@austinmacauley.com
+1 (646) 5125767

Table of Contents

Introduction

There is power in storytelling. If a story is well told, it is not only memorable but it can also change one's life or so I have found. This is a personal history, a compilation of stories that give a glimpse into who I was and am. I have changed most of the names to protect the innocent and the guilty. I invite you to enter this world, walk in my shoes, and see and feel how it was for me. These stories may be radically different from yours, yet I hope you will be able to identify the fundamental human experiences we all encounter: love, pain, spirituality, sexuality, fear, courage, living, dying, joy, tears, and laughter. As T.S. Eliot said, *Let us go then, you and I...*

Chapter One

Nonna Giussipina E Roberto [Granny And Me]

Between God and me there is no "between."

—Meister Eckhart

Nel nome del Padre, e del Figlio, e dello Spirito Santo. Amen.
[In the name of the Father, the Son, and the Holy Spirit. Amen.]

In 1948, when I was five years old, my grandmother, Giussipina, and I would say the Rosary together. We would kneel in the front porch of our Brooklyn home where an abundance of sunshine streamed through the three windows and the wooden Venetian blinds. There was pale, pink wallpaper with a repeating design of connected ribbons on a darker, but soft rose color. A chair sat against the narrow wall and the rug on the floor was deep and plush. In this tranquil setting, we prayed the Rosary in Italian.

Io credo in Dio Padre Onnipotente, creatore del cielo e della terra…
[I believe in God, the Father Almighty, Creator of heaven and earth…]

Granny, my grandmother on my mother's side, was in her fifties when I was little. She was a stout woman, with blondish, white hair that she wore in a bun. Her face was kindly and inviting, but her blue eyes revealed something within her that might be inaccessible to others. Perhaps it was a distant and lingering sadness she carried within her when she left Italy at age 13 to come to America. Perhaps it was fear spurred by the trauma of leaving the familiar to establish new ties in a place that was totally unfamiliar. She wore black because her husband, Pop, had died earlier that year when they lived on the lower east side of Manhattan. At present she was living with us: my mom and dad, my three older brothers, and me.

I wasn't in school yet and spent long days playing in the backyard or on the block with friends. It was a typical Brooklyn neighborhood and so the kids were watched constantly by our mothers to make sure we didn't get into any mischief or cross the street without the supervision of an adult. I was an outgoing kid and loved to be outside playing cowboys and Indians and riding my tricycle. I had an upholstered rocking chair in the backyard, and I would sit there endlessly rocking as my mother would look out the kitchen window and sing, "Coochi-coochi." I had a big smile on my face because my mom looked at me so adoringly and sang to me all the time as she went about her housework and her cooking. Granny had helped the family buy this house in Gravesend. She was an essential part of the household and I was the one she singled out to join her in prayer.

Padre nostro, che sei nei cieli…
[Our Father, who art in heaven…]

Granny's faith was marked by simplicity and her instructions to me about prayer were also simple,

"Roberto, talka to the God. The God, He listen to us; He lova us. He watcha over us."

She seemed to pray all day long. And she spoke to *il Signore* in Italian and taught me the prayers of the Rosary in her native tongue.

"Roberto, talka to the God anytima you wanna. He lova you."

Ave, o Maria, piena di grazia, il Signore è con te...
[Hail Mary, full of grace, the Lord is with thee....]

Granny had the rosary in the pocket of her housedress. She'd be walking about in the backyard, or through the house, or out-front fingering her beads, praying. And oftentimes, she would invite me to pray with her. How lovely and peaceful it was to be holding onto our rosary beads and praying out loud. Granny gave me my first rosary and we recited the prayers together repetitively, which lulled us into a hypnotic inner silence in the presence of our God. These moments in prayer with my grandmother were precious; the two of us in conversation with our God through Mother Mary. These moments with Granny were so serene, kneeling in the front porch, praying to this wonderful, friendly God.

Gloria al Padre, e al Figlio, e allo Spirito Santo. Come era nel principio, e ora, e sempre nei secoli dei secoli. Amen.
[Glory be to the Father, the Son, and the Holy Spirit. As it was in the beginning, is now, and ever shall be, world without end. Amen]

Believing in God was easy for me, natural. I was at home in that belief. No one else in the family was religious. My mother never went to mass. Granny was my first teacher of God. She opened the door and I happily walked through it. I knew this place...and was completely at ease there.

When my grandmother and I prayed, I began to long for something or someplace or someone I couldn't quite recall. All I knew was that I was at home with God.

Like a deer yearns for running water, so, too, do I yearn for You, O Lord. When shall I see You face to face? [Psalm 41]

I was five years old and I wanted to see God face to face. *Again.*

Chapter Two

Giussipina and Michelangelo, Francesca and Letterio, Sadie and Frank

Giussipina Papa, Granny, my grandmother on my mother's side, was blonde and blue-eyed, born in Northern Italy in 1889 and had a self-reliant nature. She thought she was a *contessa* and acted as if the world owed her something. My grandfather, Michelangelo Caputo, was olive skinned, somewhat stocky, born in Naples in 1890. He was humble, a good cook, and had an entrepreneurial spirit. Economic times were bad in Italy, so each of their families migrated south to Sicily to look for work; they didn't know each other. When the Papas and the Caputos discovered that opportunity was limited, they moved to *Bella*

America, settling in New York City's Lower East Side in the early 1900s where many relatives preceded them looking for a better life. There, Giussipina and Michelangelo met, after he opened up a bar/restaurant on the west side of Avenue A off East 11th Street. They married and had three children: two daughters and a son. My mother, Rosaria, was the oldest and she became known as Sarina and finally as Sadie. She was a spitfire.

Francesca and Letterio Scherma

My paternal grandfather, Letterio Scherma, lived in Regalbuto, Sicily with his wife and family. His wife, Francesca, prayed to St. Anthony for a boy after having six girls. She said that she would be happy if only St. Anthony would give her a boy, even if she died afterwards. Sadly, St. Anthony must have taken her offer seriously because in 1904 a boy was born whom she named Francesco. She died a month later.

In 1908, the Scherma family moved to New York City's Lower East Side to find a new life; Letterio heard that there was a large Italian population thriving there. When he arrived, he opened a grocery store on East 12th Street

16

and Avenue B and didn't send his only son, aged four, to school because he needed him to work on trucks loading and unloading food supplies. This went on for years. Apparently, Letterio hadn't heard of compulsory education or didn't care. Eventually, the authorities found out and put Francesco in school at the age of nine. He galloped through grade school and went to a technical high school and worked as an engineer without a college degree. He had a genius for things electrical and eventually was hired by Signal Engineering Inc. on Seventh Avenue and West 14th Street. He was told to sit in his office and think. By then, he was known as Frank, my dad.

Sadie and Frank

Age 16

By 1926, Frank was twenty-two and had an eye for beautiful women. When he first saw Sadie, sixteen, looking out of her second floor living room window, he was smitten. Frank was a ladies' man who had an apartment where he took women, but now he wanted to get married and have a family. He fell instantly in love with this 1920s flapper and began to woo her. She wore short lacey dresses and was a natural beauty with flowing curls. Her smile and

17

attitude captivated him. He would pass by her window each day and try to talk with her. Who was she? He had to meet her. His flirting got him nowhere; she would have none of it. She looked down her nose and told him to get lost.

Frank was an elegant gentleman. He always wore a starched white shirt with a tie and a suit when he went to business. In colder weather, he sported a topcoat and a fedora. In summer after work and on weekends, he even gardened in a white shirt and tie.

He owned the *F.A. Scherma Manufacturing Company Incorporated* at 424 Broome Street, a fifth-floor loft, in what is now known as SoHo. He had worked for years at Signal Engineering Inc., a firm which serviced General Electric and Westinghouse and other such corporations. His boss knew he could conceptualize new possibilities. That was what he was paid for. The man was a genius in the world of electrical engineering. With little formal training, he would come up with innovations that helped make his bosses lots of money. In 1953, he decided to strike out on his own with the help of Signal. He created a coaxial relay for *Ma Bell* that was in all landline telephones in the fifties. His relays went up in space through contracts with the federal government. For years, this business kept us afloat as a family in Brooklyn and got each of his four sons through college.

Frank was a *gentle* man. Soft-spoken, he was the counterpoint to Sadie, "His married lady," as we eventually called her. Sadie knew how to grandstand. She was the circus in town. She was Barnum, the showman, he was Bailey, the silent partner. As a young man, he pined for her as she sat perched on her apartment window on the Lower East Side. He would flirt with her as he passed by daily, hoping to win her favor. Even though he had a rented room where he would carry on liaisons with his paramours, he wanted Sadie.

Frank was relentless and finally got his father to speak with her father and a meeting was arranged. The families met in Sadie's apartment; Frank brought the pastries from Veniero's on East Eleventh Street. He entered their apartment with a dozen canoli, six baba cakes running with thick ricotta cream and dripping in rum and another six pasticiotta, little enclosed tarts with vanilla and chocolate pudding inside. He also brought a dozen gelatos in different flavors in case somebody wanted ice cream. He sat with his family on one side of the living room and she with hers on the other. Sadie liked the pastries and the gelato more than she liked Frank.

Frank orchestrated several chaperoned dates with both families present in her parents' flat but the relationship went nowhere fast. After a few months, Frank's oldest sister, Millie, met with Sadie.

"You know my brother is crazy about you, don't you?"

"Yeah, I know. But I'm not sure," Sadie answered.

Millie, begging, "You have to marry him, he'll be devastated if you don't. Please make our brother happy. Only you can do that, Sadie. We like you, our father likes you. *Please marry him.*"

"Okay."

It was that simple. She said yes.

And so, Francesco Scherma, age twenty-four and Rosaria Caputo, age eighteen, got married on April 29th, 1928 at Mary Help of Christians Roman Catholic Church on East Twelfth Street off Avenue A.

For several years, they lived on East Tenth Street and had two sons. Then they needed a bigger place. In 1937, they moved to the "country," better known as Brooklyn, where they had two more sons. And so, Ted, Mick, Ron, and I were born in that order. My father called me *Bobby* when I was a kid. It always made me smile.

*

After having two sons by age nineteen, Sadie said, "Enough." But the third son came seven years later and I came five years after that. Apparently, it wasn't "enough." Certainly not in Frank's eyes.

My dad used to gamble and drink with some friends down the block. When I was three years old, I remember asking my mother in what seemed like the middle of the night, "Ma, where's Daddy?"

She uttered the first thing that came to her mind, "He's out buying bananas."

Bananas? Why was he buying bananas in the middle of the night? Sadie was visibly upset. Frank's drinking and gambling eventually got out of control, and Sadie demanded he stop all that. He agreed. He stopped. Sadie was the boss.

Frank's weaknesses aside, he was beloved by all. His grandchildren affectionately called him *Pop*. Granny, living with us, had the utmost *rispetto* for him and treated him as if he were a prince. Sadie would cook up a storm for him just the way he liked it. His children wanted his approbation and competed for it.

When I was a kid, my dad would tell me stories such as the tailor who was rumored to have slain seven menacing giants in one fell swoop. Only the townspeople misheard his proclamations. He actually had slain seven flies with one swing, not seven giants. I loved that story, because it ended with him really killing seven giants!

Each and every evening, my dad would bring me a treat. One night, he forgot and I thought the world ended. I wouldn't speak to him. I thought his love was no longer mine. So, I punished him with the silent treatment, thinking I was withdrawing my love. He tried to coax me out of my despair and finally gave up. I turned away from him in bed that night, feeling guilty and hurt.

Our dog, Buddy, was a huge admirer of my dad. A mixture of Collie and German Shepherd, he entered the household in 1948 and automatically attached to my dad. Buddy would wait by the basement window each and every night where my dad would pass on the way back from work. He would pace back and forth if Dad were late. When he arrived, he would run upstairs and jump on him in utter joy because his master had come home!

Sadie couldn't understand why the dog didn't revere her. After all, *she* fed him, cleaned his eyes, gave him water, brushed his hair. However, the heart wants what it wants. My father really did nothing for Buddy, but his heart belonged to Daddy. One time, my dad was in the hospital for three weeks. Each evening, Buddy would wait for him to come home and when he didn't, he would make whimpering sounds for over an hour. We had to comfort him, but he would not be comforted. When Dad returned home from the hospital, you would have thought it was the Second Coming; such was the joy that Buddy displayed.

Frank had a quieter presence in the household compared to Sadie. But when I got into trouble, it was my dad who went to school to fight for me. He assured my homeroom teacher, Miss Fitzpatrick, that I would behave and she believed him. His temperate ways disarmed many, including me.

He was never disappointed with me and always supported my next venture. On the day I left the seminary, he greeted me with, "Welcome home, Robert!" When I brought my live-in girlfriend Ana home, he said, "I'm glad to meet you. You're as beautiful as my son said." When I announced I was gay, he said, "You're my son and I love you. I want you to be happy." When he met my lifetime partner, he took Beryl's outstretched hand with *both* his hands and said, "I'm happy to meet you."

Sadie was a cheekier presence who had no compunctions about asserting her opinions. She wasn't so thrilled with my choices.

Play high school football, no!
Become a priest, no!
Leave home and move to the city, no!
Live with a girlfriend, no!
Be gay, Absolutely not!

Yet, she gave into each move I made and then supported them. Sadie had met her match. I took after her.

Chapter Three
Sadie

My mom, Sadie, always lit up the room. My friends adored her. She always had a smile on her face and you could hear her singing as she cleaned each room, winding up in the kitchen, her last stop. As freewheeling as she appeared, she had her rules. This was a woman in charge of her domain. She was the matriarch of the family and in charge of all domestic affairs. There were only two choices: abide by her rules or rebel against them. As the family grew, daughters-in-law knew that they had to gain her favor. They chose to accede to her reign.

As my mom cleaned, she would allow me to play in the kitchen until she appeared there with Fuller Brush mop in hand. I had to stop, put my toys away, and Sadie, the cleaning machine, took over. I was moved to a chair where I had to sit until the floor wax dried. I listened to the soap operas on the radio like *The Romance of Helen Trent,* which taught me that because a woman is 35 or more, "romance in life need not be over." Later, when we had a house, Sadie could maneuver me into the backyard or if it rained, downstairs in the basement. To Sadie, cleanliness really was next to godliness.

One fine spring day, we were sitting in the backyard of the family home and somehow the subject of God came up. Sadie wasn't particularly Catholic, never went to mass, and certainly had no need of priests. But today, she was pondering the existence of God as she looked at the vegetable garden, which my father tended to so assiduously.

"It's amazing. You plant some tomatoes and peppers and corn and string beans in the backyard. And then you take some horseshit and put it around the plants and presto! You have vegetables. How can anyone *not* believe in God?"

The move to Brooklyn became a family trend. My aunt, Zia Concetta, lived around the corner from my family's house and Zia Maria lived a few blocks away. After a while, Sadie's first cousin, Anita, and her husband, Willy, decided to migrate as well. They got an apartment five minutes away. Anita and Sadie were best friends and Anita visited Sadie every day *after* the house was cleaned.

One day, Anita came over and said to Sadie, "I want to open a bank account. They gave me this card to fill out."

Sadie poured two cups of coffee; they sat down at the kitchen table and proceeded to fill out the form.

Now, you've got to know that these two first cousins were Lower East Siders, born and bred, back when the Lower East side was a slum, and while they had street smarts, they didn't have the other kind. Even so, Sadie was the intellect of the two; after all, she graduated from the eighth grade while Anita dropped out after the sixth. It was only fitting that Anita should consult with Sadie. Those two years of post-graduate education apparently made a difference. At least that's what Sadie always told her.

They started filling out the card. At first it was easy: first name, last name, address, borough, zone number, city. A cinch. Then it became a little more complicated.

Anita said, "All right, it says *Husband,* so I'll put down *Willy.* Right?"

Sadie nodded approval.

"Now, it says *Father's name.*"

Perplexed, Anita asked, "Now, do they want *my* father's name or the father of my children?"

Anita decided they obviously didn't want her father's name, so she put Willy's name down again.

"Sadie, what do they mean by *Bus Address*?"

Bus Address? Sadie thought for a nano-second and said authoritatively, "Put down the Kings Highway bus."

As she's writing down the *Kings Highway Bus,* Anita, indignant, asks, "And what if I want to take *the Avenue U* bus? Goddamn it. Or *the 86th Street* bus? And what the hell is it their business *what* bus I take?"

"I don't know what to tell ya. Leave the card here. I'll ask Frank tonight when he gets home."

After all, Frank ran his own business, had dealings with General Electric, and even invented a relay component that was shot into space. Surely, he could decipher the hidden meaning of the bus address inquiry.

So, Frank comes home after a hard day's work. Anita had gone and left the form with Sadie. Sadie posed the problem to him. He seemed baffled, confused.

"Bus address? Bus address? Let me see the application."

After surveying the application, Frank declared triumphantly, "It's not *Bus Address.* It's *Business* Address. Don't you see the dot?"

"Oh, yeah, yeah…"

And so, Frank saved the day, as usual. He quipped aloud what I'd heard him say a hundred times before, "You know, Sadie, you could confuse the whole Coxey Army."

Sadie also had a talent for malapropisms. Once, sensing that I was too much of a maverick with a penchant for rabble-rousing in my new job, Sadie admonished me.

"Robert, don't upset the apricots."

Like the Sicilian mother in *Cinema Paradiso*, Sadie was free with her hands when angry with me. I was smacked across the face regularly up until puberty when I wouldn't take it anymore. Today, it would be considered child abuse. Then it was run of the mill discipline in our neighborhood.

We had a storage trunk in the basement on which all our shoes were neatly placed. That's two pairs of *shoes each for* my four brothers and two pairs for my dad. One day, Sadie and I were having an argument; something I did or said enraged her.

"You son of a bitch!"

From the other side of the basement, I shouted at her, "You know, Ma, you're calling yourself a bitch!"

My observation only infuriated her more.

"Ooooh, you bastard! I'll get you!"

I didn't have time to tell her that she was maligning herself again as she went over to the trunk and proceeded to throw twenty shoes at me, one at a time.

She had a lousy aim and I ducked each and every assault.

"Pick up those shoes!"

"No! You're just going to throw them at me again."

"Pick up those goddamn shoes... I won't throw them at you."

I knew she was setting me up for the kill.

Still, I handed her the first shoe and she tried to whack me with it. She missed.

"See, I can't trust you! I'm not picking them up until you leave."

One thing Sadie couldn't tolerate was a mess. Shoes all over the place! She looked at me askance and went upstairs cursing under her breath. She knew I'd put each shoe back in pairs and do so neatly. I took after her—I was compulsively neat as well.

I thought to myself, *I'm living with a crazy woman. Good thing she's a great cook, otherwise I'd have to kill her.*

Sadie's cleaning routine had strict guidelines. Everything was done each day, twice. Floors with rugs were vacuumed and then again later on. The same with washing the linoleum covered floors. All bedrooms were aired out and beds remade. Every item in the house was dusted; furniture, lamps, blinds, everything. She was always running downstairs doing several laundries and putting them out on the clothesline in the backyard to dry. One day, I was sitting in the kitchen as Sadie was cleaning the other rooms.

A set of encyclopedias was in the back porch off the kitchen. I was five and I got a volume or two. I started looking through one and came across a statue of Venus De Milo. No arms, but she had tits!

I stared at the statue and was fascinated. *So, this is what's underneath a woman's blouse.* I had three older brothers and my dad for company, so tits were not available. Only my mom's and that's not right. Venus's tits fascinated me. I rested my head on my hand and just stared and stared and stared. Sadie entered the kitchen and exited several times. Every once in a while, she smiled at me and sung out, "Coochi-choochi," as she proceeded to the next task. I didn't look up; I was busy.

After a while, Sadie noticed that I was transfixed, staring at something in this book. She finally stopped behind me and saw what I was preoccupied by.

"Oh, my God, what are you looking at?"

I looked up and shrugged my shoulder as she snatched the book from under my nose.

"Do something else!"

I didn't want to do something else. But that was the end of that; the tits-police had confiscated the evidence and I sat there bewildered. I thought, *Did I do something wrong?*

Angie

When I was eight, my Aunt Angie, Uncle Ray, and Cousin Robert moved in upstairs. Angie and Sadie were sisters. We built an addition on the second floor so that now there were two more bedrooms. Granny moved into one of them and Robert in the other. Uncle Ray had multiple sclerosis and worked part-time from home as a jeweler and Aunt Angie worked at *Lady Suzanne Brassieres* in Bay Ridge, where she was the shop steward.

Aunt Angie was tough, outspoken, a film *noir* Barbara Stanwyck type of dame who wasn't afraid of anyone. Blonde, cigarette dangling from her lips, sexy as all get-out, she would walk down the street to the bus in her stiletto heels. If she saw a teenager on a bus intimidating an older woman, she would step in and say, "See that window there? If you don't cut it out, I'll put you right through it!" The teen would freeze in her tracks, knowing she meant it.

If a man was frightening a young woman with unwanted touching on the subway and Angie got a whiff of it, picking whatever name came to mind, she shouted out, "*Susan! Susan*! Come over here by me." And *Susan* would meekly come over and Angie would give a dirty look to the guy who was harassing her.

In the early 1960s, she was on a Utica Avenue bus on her way to visit her husband, Ray, who was now living with full-blown M.S. at Jewish Chronic Disease Hospital in Brooklyn. Angie was the only white person on the bus when it braked suddenly and she accidentally bumped into a woman who was black. The woman got angry, looked directly at Angie and said,

"White trash!"

My aunt turned around and directly looked her in the eyes and retorted,

"Black trash!"

The bus passengers started to clap menacingly. Angie was defiant and ready for a fight. The other woman backed off. She was fearless in the face of adversity and always fought for the underdog even when it was her.

I thought she deserved a song. So, one day, I wrote her a song, "Angela, my Angela, sweet Angela, lah dee dah."

I sang it to her when I was avoiding doing college calculus assignments or an essay that had to be written. I'd sit at the bottom of her stairwell and simply sing this refrain with my guitar, over and over. She laughed and laughed as she continued about her day.

My much-loved Aunt Angie was also religious in her own way. She would say, "A lot of people pray to the Holy Saints or Our Blessed Mother. Not me; I go *directly* to *Our Lord*."

One Saturday, we decided to go to confession at Saints Simon and Jude church down the block. In those days. people went to confession often. So, we were in the church and waited on line for Father McGrail. He was the pastor and a gruff old guy who always kinda barked at you. And he had a nose so vast that the kids in the neighborhood would exclaim, "Eek, Eek! What a beak!"

Aunt Angie was ahead of me in line and confessed first. I could hear them both because they spoke clearly and loudly.

"Bless me, Father, for I have sinned. It has been two weeks since my last confession," Angie started. And then, "I have no sins."

"Come now, you *must* have some sins!"

"No, I don't," she asserted.

"Do you lie?"

"Oh, I tell little white lies, but those are not sins."

"Oh, yes, they are!"

"*Oh, no, they're not!*"

"Miss, you're deluding yourself!"

"Father, I'm getting out of here. You're absolutely wrong. When I tell a little white lie, I'm making sure someone doesn't get hurt."

"You can't do that! That's a sin."

"I'm outta here. This is ridiculous. The very idea… What nerve you have!"

She was beside herself as she approached me. I suggested she go to Father Johnson, who was a gentler soul.

On the way home, Aunt Angie said, "Now *that's* my kinda priest. Father Johnson told me to forget what Father McGrail said and just tell him my confession. I told him about white lies and he just listened and told me to say five Hail Marys and five Our Fathers. I feel much better."

Whenever Italian Sadie wanted to get the latest news on the block, she would sit on the front stoop of our Brooklyn home at 33 Van Sicklen Street. As soon as Irish Winnie came out of her home across the street at 46 Van Sicklen Street, Sadie would call her over. Winnie was my best friend Ken's mother. By virtue of their girth and commanding manner, Sadie and Winnie were looming presences in the neighborhood.

"Winnie, come on over," Sadie beckoned.

"Hi, Sadie, I'll be over in a minute," Winnie, a plus-sized woman in a bathing suit, turned off the hose, stopped washing down the walk, and crossed over to Sadie.

They exchanged pleasantries.

"So, what's going on with that woman next door to you?" Sadie inquired.

Winnie answered, "You mean that goddamned mountain Guinea? Well, you know, she's got a big mouth and…"

Sadie interrupted, "Winnie, I don't like the word *Guinea*..."

"Oh, Sadie, I don't mean you. I mean that goddamned mountain Guinea next door to me."

"But, Winnie, I really don't like that word."

"You're right, Sadie," and after a breath continued, "and so that goddamned mountain Guinea next door to me is such a nuisance..."

Sadie let her go on; knowing that there was no curtailing an unstoppable force such as Winnie. Resigned to this fact, Sadie let political correctness take a back seat to the important task of the day; getting the latest dirt on the block.

Ted

My oldest brother, Ted, resembled Marlon Brando and could be a little menacing like Stanley Kowalski. He was a tough guy in a 1950s kind of way and took no crap from anyone. He was an all-city baseball player and enjoyed the limelight. Cocky and sure of himself, Ted thought the sun rose and set on him; or as we said in the Gravesend section of Brooklyn, he thought his shit didn't stink.

One day, Ted and I were down in the basement, alone. He was turning nineteen and I was five. He was reading a sports magazine with his feet up on the table, a mortal sin in my mother's house. I was on the floor, playing with my cherished toy bus. Not looking up from his magazine, Ted issued a command.

"Get me a glass of water!"

With my big brown eyes, I looked up at him and pondered the situation. I knew I was pissed and wasn't going to do it.

"Get it yourself. What are you, a cripple? I'm not your slave."

He gave me the look of death; *my death* and the fury of hell was let loose.

In clipped tones, he said, "Get…me…a…glass…of water… Now!"

Again, my heart racing, "No! Get it yourself!"

He leapt up and tried to grab me. I ran under the antique dining room table, the one he had his feet on, and easily escaped his grasp. When he almost got me by the back of my tee shirt; I decided to call in the artillery.

"Ma, Ted is chasing me! Ma! Ma!"

We could hear Sadie's voice from upstairs.

"What's going on down there?"

Ted said, "Nothing."

I countered, "Ma, get down here! Quick!"

So Sadie, a woman whose belly entered the room before she did, came clomping down the stairs and asked, "What the hell is going on here?"

I said, "He wants me to get him a glass of water. I told him no."

By this time, I was clinging to my mother's leg, holding on for dear life. Ted looked at her and then at me and then back at her.

Sadie looked directly at Ted and said, "You big stiff! Get your own water. You don't tell him what to do!"

One corner of my mouth started to curl upwards. Then Sadie laid down the law, "If anybody's going to order this kid around, it's gonna be me, not you!"

My eyes opened wide and I realized that the natural order of things had been restored. Ted glared at me and warned me that he'd get me later.

"Over my dead body!" Sadie warned.

That day I stuck to my mother like glue.

As a teenager, I always liked to play my music, loud. My family had a Webcor multi-speed phonograph, the latest model that played my LPs in High Fidelity using an expensive diamond needle. It was located in our newly renovated basement and my 20-year-old brother, Ron, and I shared control over the turntable on alternate days. I was 15 at the time.

The basement window closest to the street was open so that passersby could readily hear my latest L.P. On my day, I'd play the likes of *West Side Story* or Ray Charles or Ella Fitzgerald or Nina Simone or Johnny Mathis or Frank Sinatra at the highest volume, assuming that the whole neighborhood of Italians and Jews and Poles and Greeks and Germans would certainly want to hear my latest record acquisition.

Sadie, for the most part, enjoyed the music, and I would hear her singing along with the American standards she recognized. One day, she sang along with Old Blue Eyes as he churned out Cole Porter's *I've Got You Under My Skin*. She sang, "Use your mentality, wake up to reality…"

She asked me, "What's *mentality*?"

I answered, "Ma, it's something you haven't got."

Sadie loved the music but was always complaining about the volume. From upstairs, I would hear, "It's too loud! Turn it down!"

"Okay, Ma."

I'd turn it down initially, but slowly turned it up louder and louder.

After several such interactions, she would warn, "I'm going to come down and cut the cord!"

"All right, Ma, all right!" I was annoyed. How could the neighbors or I enjoy the music if it was a whisper? Little by little, I would up the volume till it was full blast again.

This routine would ensue again and again, but one day she threatened, "The music is too loud! I'm coming down with the scissors!"

"Yeah, yeah," I muttered as I heard her running down the stairs and yes, with a pair of scissors! I was on the other side of the basement when she ran over to the Webcor and actually cut the wire!

Boom! Some smoke rose up and Sadie exclaimed, "Look what you made me do!"

"I didn't make you do anything! You're a crazy person. What's the matter with you?"

"I'll come over there and smack you around no matter how old you are! You made me do this! It's your fault!"

I didn't always call my mom Sadie. When I was attending Brooklyn College, I took a course in the philosophical foundations of education.

"Today, let's discuss parents," Professor Maxine Greene said to us, her young adult students. "At your ages of nineteen, twenty, and twenty-one, you no longer need parents as such. You're becoming independent. In that maturation process, it's a good idea to reconceive your relationship with your parents as *friends*."

Made sense to me.

So, I went home after classes that day and brought up the topic at dinner. It was a Thursday, so we were having ziti with my mother's homemade marinara sauce with fresh basil from the backyard. The pecorino Romano was speckled with black peppercorns ready to be grated when needed. The eggplant was fried in three ways; paper thin and plain, breaded, and breaded sandwiched with sauce, mozzarella, and ricotta fresca. She fried meatballs that were oval in shape and smothered them in fried onions. There was also a huge salad with her fabulous seasoning. She used olive oil, oregano, salt, pepper, fresh garlic, and red wine vinegar, and mixed the salad with her hands.

It was just the three of us; my mom, my dad, and me. My three older brothers were married and out of the house.

I opened with, "Mom, Dad, today in class my professor said we should reconceive our relationships with our parents, that at this age we no longer needed a mother or a father. We're all adults, let's be friends. I think it's a good idea."

Their jaws dropped. I concluded, "So, from now on, it's *Sadie* and *Frank*."

Sadie raised her eyebrows and opened her mouth and said, "Get the hell outta here! What are you nuts? I'll still smack you across the face no matter how big you are."

Frank just smiled, took it in stride, and continued to eat, no, *swallow,* his specially prepared Ronzoni number nine spaghettini; he could only eat spaghetti-type pasta, otherwise he'd choke. Really.

Speaking to Sadie, I said, "Nope. Sorry. From now on, it's Sadie and Frank."

I needed the Pecorino Romano, "Sadie, would you please pass me the cheese?"

Sadie bit her lip, gave a look to kill, and passed the cheese and the grater.

She looked over to Frank and said, "I'm gonna kill that kid. Why does he come home with these crazy ideas? Where did we go wrong?"

One day, maybe ten years later, I decided to visit Sadie for a cup of coffee. I hadn't seen her in a while. I also needed cash.

Now, Sadie always had a secret stash of money in the second dresser drawer in her bedroom, under some handkerchiefs. My brother, Ron, and I would always borrow some, pay her back, borrow some more. After all, to go to the bank, wait on long lines, cash a personal check, and show identification was a colossal pain in the neck. There were no A.T.M. machines back then.

Sipping my coffee, I said, "Ma, I need some money. Can I borrow $50?"

In an instant, she replied, "Oh, now it's *Ma*?

*

It was a Tuesday night; Sadie, Frank, my brothers, Ted, Mick, and their wives, and Ron with his wife-to-be were home for dinner. I was 16 at the time, a high school senior at Lafayette High School, home of crooner Vic Damone and baseball's Joe Pepitone and Sandy Koufax. It was our every Tuesday night dinner with the usual cast of characters including a guest appearance from Aunt Angie who lived upstairs and came down after dinner for a cup of coffee.

We already had our fresh-made wedding soup with meatballs and Orzo and devoured most of the six pounds of veal cutlets. What was left over was for sandwiches the next day. Sadie ordered the veal cutlets as thin as could be from Sal the butcher on Avenue S, breaded them with her own special seasoning and fried them one after another. Spinach sautéed with garlic and olive oil and the huge salad were gone. There was hardly any bread left. But now, it was time for fresh fennel and nuts.

Sadie was up to mischief; you could see it in her eyes and that grin she had slapped across her face. She especially loved to embarrass us. She stood at the head of the table and with a large chef's knife, she pointed at each of her sons and husband and started the inquisition.

"Let's see. How many nuts do we have at this table? Ted, two. Ron, two. Rob, two. Mick, two. Frank, two. That makes ten. Wait. It's a miscount!"

She started again, "Ted, two. Ron, two. Rob, two. *Mick, three!* Frank, two. That makes eleven. Now we've got it right!"

My brother, Mickey, was reputed to have three testicles or what appeared to be three testicles. Family legend had it that two were functioning, one was not. Mickey just rolled his eyes at this accounting once again and, exasperated, sighed, "Ma, *really*?"

Sadie crossed over the line much too often. Once in a while, as one of her teenaged sons was climbing the stairs and she was a step or two behind, Sadie would goose us! I would say, "Ma, stop it."

With a smattering of Freud under my belt, I'd say, "This is very Oedipal, except in reverse."

She just gave me a dismissive dirty look and continued climbing the stairs.

One time, I blurted out that she was hot for her sons! She chased me around the basement and up the stairs, but luckily, I was too fast for her.

This woman thought our genitals and our buttocks were her province.

"After all," she would often say, "I made them!"

Mickey was blond haired at birth apparently a genetic transmission from Granny, Sadie's mother, who was from Northern Italy, where blond and blue-eyed was the norm. With our dad's Sicilian background, Mickey's eyes were hazel, an oddity in our brown-eyed family. His hair caught up; brown by the time he reached puberty. Mickey was my second oldest brother, we were twelve years apart. Sadie was upset when he was born as she was with each of us, "Goddammit, I got caught again."

Mickey was the brother I had the most fun with.

"How about a Manhattan?" he'd ask.

"Absolutely! Get out the maraschino cherries!" I'd say. Mick made the best Manhattans and when he offered, I was always up for one. Or two.

Mickey, in his early 20s, announced, "Let's have a party!" He organized a huge event in our driveway and backyard in Brooklyn for some thirty friends. There were lanterns and music and liquor and lots of finger-eating foods. It was a gala event and when I was little I enjoyed the fun of it watching from the back-porch window, big-eyed and smiling.

At age seventeen, I was old enough to party. One night I'd managed to get Sadie and Frank and Angie to go out so I could hold a big bash to celebrate my high school graduation. We were all drinking and creating mass mayhem when they unexpectedly returned home! They heard shouts coming from the basement and Sadie yelled down, "What's going on down there?"

"Nothing, Mom, it's all okay. Don't worry. We'll make less noise."

Only a few minutes later, there was another uproar that caused not only Sadie to be concerned, but also my dad and Aunt Angie. From the top of the stairs, Sadie shouted, "Something's going on down there! What is it?"

"Mom, I'm sorry. We got drunk and people are passing out."

Aunt Angie said, "I'll make coffee!"

By now, one boy was sick and vomiting, *thank God in the toilet,* and he could use some coffee.

"Does he like it with milk and sugar?"

Rolling my eyes, I said, "Black coffee will do fine."

Sadie, when hearing that two of the girls were smashed, too, said, "Bring them over to Winnie. She knows how to handle drunks. After all, the Irish know about these things."

By 9:30 p.m. the evening had wound down, the liquor bottles and beer cans confiscated, the music discontinued, the gang subdued.

When everyone left, Sadie laid down the law, "That's the last time you'll have a party for a long, long time. The next time you drink, the next day I'll be drinking at your funeral. Believe me!"

I believed her.

I was the last of her four sons, also the last teenager she had to contend with. Dealing with my unruliness proved to be hazardous to her health and mine.

*

One time, Mickey and one of our first cousins, Alfred, also in his 20s, were talking. I was nearby.

"You know what I did yesterday?" asked Alfred.

"What?" queried Mickey.

"I went to *seven* movies!" answered Alfred.

"Seven! I've done two or three, but never seven in a row!"

Overhearing this, it sounded great. I vowed that I would do that when I grew up. As an adult, I do just that. I can sit in the Angelica Movie Theater and snatch up five tickets for five shows and be in heaven! Never quite made seven.

It was Tuesday night at my Mom and Dad's house again. That meant that all the brothers and their girlfriends came to dinner. Mickey was sitting next to me and I was enjoying the thinly pounded cutlets and the green salad that was luscious and succulent and superbly seasoned and the French fries, which I left for last. I had a few more, which I was just about to eat, when my brother, Ron, engaged me in conversation. I turned away and when I returned to my plate, Mickey had absconded with my last fries and devoured them. I wanted to *kill* him! Yeah, it's *great* to have brothers!

Mickey had such a great tenor voice that he was offered lead singer for Freddy Martin swing band in the forties, which he didn't pursue. Always in a choir, he married Delia, who had a lovely and lilting soprano voice. On their honeymoon in December 1954 at the Eden Roc resort in Miami, both appeared on a radio show where they sang several popular standards. They were offered a contract, which they refused. Family lore has it that they could have been another Edie Gormé and Steve Lawrence. They had good looks and wonderful voices that worked well together. The simple life, however, was calling them.

Ron

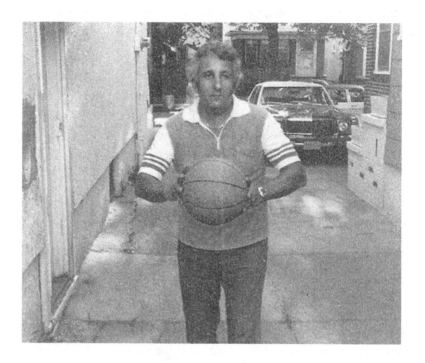

We all worried about our weight, especially Ron, who was five years older than me. We used to jog a mile, marvel at that accomplishment, and then walk back the mile smoking Pall Malls. We spoke about life and love and everything in between. We were on an exercise jaunt, to fight the good fight against weight gain. Every Scherma brother was on a diet now and again, including or especially, me.

It probably was in our genes. Sadie certainly was rotund although Frank was thin. She complained, "I blame Frank. He never told me I was getting fat."

One day, Sadie, Ron, and I were sitting at the kitchen table at the house in Brooklyn. We were having a cup of coffee. With Sweet 'n Low, of course. Ron, at the time, was gaining weight; I was losing. Ron decided to get up from the table, go over to the refrigerator, and take a look at what goodies might be calling him. This took all of ten seconds.

While this was going on, Sadie turned to me and said, "Look at your brother! He's a *mountain*."

I said, "Ma, be quiet; he'll hear you!"

Softly, she asked, "You know what your brother's problem is?"

"No, Ma, what?"

Sadie, looking downhearted and forlorn, gave her pronouncement. Shaking her head back and forth she said, "*He likes to eat.*"

*

"Ma, did you ever have an orgasm?"

Perhaps it was because my mother and I were on reclining chairs in the classic psychoanalytic position recalling the Freudian dictum, "Say anything," that I asked that question.

"What kind of a question is that?" Sadie asked.

"Well, have you?" I pressed and Sadie responded, "No, no. Not at all. How disgusting! Have an orgasm? My God…"

Then she recalled something out of the far recesses of her mind, "But there was this one time no, no, no. Only once. Men are hot bastards!"

In the mid-1970s, the sexual revolution was at its height and the goal of every heterosexual couple was to orgasm together. My mother's worldview about sex was, "Let your husband do what he has to, put up with it, and don't like it!"

Sadie was a true exponent of her time, *but there was that one time…*

I said, "Sadie, that's terrific. At least there was that one time. Could happen again, no?"

"No! *Never*. Let's change the subject."

*

One time Frank was criticizing Sadie and she spoke out, "Frank, you're always knocking me down! Just once I'd like to see you knock me up."

39

Frank and Sadie changed their double mattress to queen size. At the dinner table Sadie commented, "Frank, that extra six inches in bed makes a world of difference!'

*

Thanksgiving 1979

The truth about my birth came out at a typical Scherma family holiday meal, which was pandemonium as usual. Thirty people, including Sadie who was chief chef, Frank, me and my brothers and their families, several of our friends and Aunt Angie sat around a set of long tables. It was Thanksgiving 1979. The youngest kids were placed nearby at a separate table. There was always too much food and the wine flowed readily. So did the conversation. The current topic was about having children. Sadie and her younger sister, Angie, were speaking. I was sitting nearby.

"You need to have four or five kids to understand what it means to be a mother," Sadie said.

"So, I only had one, then my husband got sick," countered Aunt Angie. Her husband not only had M.S. but he had died prematurely in 1966 at age fifty-two.

Karen, a niece, said, "You need a man around the house, Aunt Ang."

"Get the hell outta here!" said Angie.

Sadie, speaking to Karen, her grandchild, said, "Sweetheart, you said you wanted the twisted bread and butter. It's right there. Pass this to your daughter, Mickey."

Sadie continued, speaking to me, "Your father saw me give birth to Ted and said, 'Never again, Sadie, never again!'"

I asked, "How did he see you?"

"I gave birth at home."

Someone chimed in, "Sure while they were making pasta fazoula."

"No," said Sadie, "they were in the kitchen making Jewish cheesecake… The nurse was showing them how to make Jewish cheesecake."

My friend Jim, Jewish, laughed out loud.

Angie said, "I was standing outside the bedroom. I was on watch."

Sadie continued, "Frank said to me that after Ted, 'Never again, Sadie, never again,' and one year later, I got caught again. And he told me, *'Never.'"*

"Ma, how did you feel when I was born?" I, the fourth son, inquired.

"You were a big mistake. All the baths I took. Soaped myself, burnt myself. And the mustard plasters…"

I whispered to my sister-in-law, Gloria, in an aside, "My shrink didn't believe me. Now he will." I was recording this whole conversation on audiotape, documenting family events as I always did. Family barbecues, family events are all on tape. I would go from person to person like a roving reporter. Now I had evidence. My shrink, who was always laughing and astonished when I told him my Sadie stories, would now have to take them very seriously.

Sadie, relentless, continued, "For four or five months I couldn't accept it and I was fighting with my husband… He couldn't say a word to me. You'd be surprised how angry I was that I was pregnant again."

Gloria, having fun needling her, said, "So, you took it out on Dad. And where were you when it happened?"

"Well, it was his fault!"

Gloria, "Why was it his fault?"

"Because it was his fault!" a victimized Sadie asserted.

"But you were there!" said Gloria.

"No, sir, no, sir. It doesn't take *two* to tango. You can get caught."

"Yeah, but you enjoyed it," countered Gloria, my brother Ted's wife.

"I wish we had the pill in those days!"

Sadie continued, "And you know the funny thing is that when I gave birth to Robert, I didn't want to go to the doctor. The doctor knew how I felt about doctors."

She turned to her oldest grandson, Frank, aged twenty-two, who said, "But, Grandmother, you have to go to the doctor for blood tests."

"Well, you're right," she replied. "The doctor insisted I go for blood tests. I went once and then I told him I'd call him when I was ready to give birth."

Gloria, stunned, asked, "You had *one* blood test and then you gave birth?"

Sadie, making it perfectly clear, said, "When I needed him, I called him and then I gave birth."

"So, was Ronny unexpected, too?"

He was the third son.

Sadie explained, "Yes. I was scared, 'Oh no, another child…' I already had Mickey and Ted; one was nine and the other twelve."

Ronny, in the background, was starting a food fight with the nieces and nephews. He had already wreaked havoc when he knifed the container of milk on two sides and pools of milk were collecting on the breakfast table. He also took the carving knife when the twenty-one-pound turkey was placed on the table and stabbed it saying, "Now, we can eat it. It's dead."

Sadie pleaded, "Ronny, Ronny, don't throw bread... *That kid!*"

Ronny was forty-one years old at the time, but at family celebrations, we all regressed to childhood.

Gloria, going back to the topic at hand, asked, "You got pregnant with Ronny and you weren't happy, right?"

"No, I wasn't happy. After I had Ted and Mickey... Remember I was *nineteen*! I said, 'No more children.' But a year later, I got caught again and I had an abortion and I got rid of that. And then a year later, I had another abortion. I said, 'What the hell is going on? What...am I going to have one baby after another?'"

She looked around the table, searching out for Frank, my father, her husband, "That bastard! Where is he?"

Some people are anal retentive; Sadie was oral expulsive. Whatever went through her mind came right out of her mouth.

Now, most of us knew this story. Sadie had two kids, then two abortions, then two more kids. But her sister, Angie, was hearing this for the first time. As close as they were, they harbored secrets from each other.

Startled, Angie asked, "You had an *abortion*?"

No answer.

Then again, incredulous, Angie said to everyone at the table, "My sister had an abortion?"

She asked Sadie again, "You had an *abortion*?"

Sadie answered triumphantly, "Two!"

"And your husband allowed you to do this?" Angie asked.

"Why not?"

"You killed two kids!" Angie shouted in disbelief.

"I killed two kids? You mean I killed two *bloods*," Sadie retorted, always the graphic one.

"Oh...no...Sadie, no."

In righteous rage, "Come on, I would've had six kids... I would've gone crazy."

"Who took you for these abortions?" Angie asked.

"My sister-in-law."

"Your sister-in-law is *no damn good*," said Angie, "I don't believe this."

Sadie reasserted, "I only got rid of *bloods*."

With this exit line, Sadie announced that she needed to go to the bathroom and excused herself.

*

A couple of days later, I visited Sadie; we were alone.

"So, Sadie, you tried to have me aborted several times? Is that really true?"

We were sitting at the kitchen table, each sipping a fresh cup of coffee from the electric Farberware percolator.

"Yes, I didn't want any more kids. I couldn't stand it. You were a mistake," she said for the umpteenth time.

"Sadie, do you know how it feels to be referred to as *a mistake*?" I asked.

"You were all mistakes. Not just you," Sadie clarified.

"I know. You've been telling us that all our lives. Don't you realize what a terrible thing that is to say to a son? It made me feel unwanted and unloved. And that's how I went into the world feeling, unwanted and unloved."

"Oh, no, Robert. That wasn't it at all."

"Still, Ma, it wasn't a good thing to say," I asserted.

"I know, I know. I was crazed. It was late 1942, the middle of the war. Your father was working all kinds of hours and was starting to gamble and maybe drink too much. I had three kids and I was scared."

"Yeah, Ma, go on."

Sadie continued, "When I found out I was pregnant, I was beside myself. I didn't tell your father but I tried to get rid of you with sitz baths, saline solutions, a whole bunch of things. Nothing worked. And then...."

"And then what, Ma?"

"And then you were born. And as soon as I saw your beautiful face, I fell in love with you."

I didn't know whether to give her a big hug or slap her across the face. I said, "Ma, you never told me this part of the story...the *important* part. Instead of feeling unwanted and unloved, I could have felt wanted and loved. Why didn't you tell me this earlier?" I implored.

"I don't know why. I thought I did. But apparently, I didn't," Sadie answered in a soft and apologetic tone.

Well, I was in my 36th year and Sadie was in her 69th. Why couldn't she have told me this thirty years ago? I could have avoided all those years of misery and feeling the outsider. Somebody ought to write that goddamned *parents' manual* already and give it out when a child is born.

"All I know is that from the first moment I saw you, I loved you," Sadie reiterated.

My father was equally undemonstrative. The same year, he went into the hospital for some serious ailment. As he entered the O.R., he yelled out,

"Tell Sadie *this is it*!"

A day later, he told us, "Tell Sadie this isn't it."

We were relieved.

But when I thought he could be dying, I asked my father a question that always plagued me.

Softly, I asked, "Dad, do you love me?"

I didn't know. How could I have known my dad all these years and not know?

He paused a moment deep in thought. Then he spoke.

"Robert, I have *always* loved you."

It broke my heart.

Why hadn't I known? My dad, like my mom, hadn't let me in on the secret until now. Or was I just not listening? Or not seeing what was obvious to others and to them?

Sadie, "From the first moment I saw you, I loved you."

Frank, "Robert, I have *always* loved you."

Love was always there and now it was recovered, no, uncovered. And for this, I was grateful as I underwent a seismic shift in my perception of who I was.

Chapter Four

School Days

Living in a house with my cousin, my aunt, and uncle, and my grandmother upstairs and the six of us downstairs was a mixed blessing. We were always visiting each other, having meals or barbecues together, celebrating holidays under the same roof. Through the years, my cousin and I grew up in that household and became brothers in the process. While it was mostly positive, for me, it did have its drawbacks.

My cousin, Robert, was nine, a year older than me when he moved in. Slowly, I changed. From an outgoing, swashbuckling kind of kid with lots of friends, I became fearful and unsure of myself. I felt that everyone in my family treated my cousin better than me.

"After all, his father has M.S. and he's on call all the time. He needs more than you."

And he got more than me. At Christmas time, he always got more gifts than I did. If there was an extra dessert, I would hear, "Save it for Robert upstairs."

I thought to myself, *What about Robert downstairs?* I was furious. Little by little, it seemed he took over my friends. I felt they liked the new kid on the block more than me and I, being hurt, took a back seat.

How could I say anything? Who would listen? He was my cousin and I did like him and he had a bad deal because his dad had M.S. We'd be in the park playing handball, or in the street tossing a Spalding, and every half-hour he had to report home to see if his father needed anything. It was torture for him and so I couldn't say a damn thing. I turned inwards and became embittered, silently. I soon wouldn't leave the house, except for school and church.

At the same time, a succession of bullies plagued me in grade school and in junior high. My lack of self-esteem became easily detectible. I was an easy mark. First, there was this guy, Jerry, who was in my third-grade class, the year after my cousin moved upstairs. Jerry and his henchman, Tony, would follow me after school.

"I like that pen in your pocket," Jerry would say.

"Yeah, so do I," parroted Tony, "Give it to me."

I gave it.

"You got any money?" Jerry asked.

"Yes."

"Give it to me."

I forked over the nickel and the pennies I had.

"Do as we say and you won't get hurt," said Tony.

This happened several times a week so I started delaying my departure from school and found other ways to go home. Third grade was torture. In fourth and fifth grade, there was relief. I was smart and funny and a popular kid. I became friendly with a kid named Frank. He was tall and a good athlete. For three weeks out of every year, gym was suspended and we learned what only Arthur Murray could teach: the fox trot, the rumba, and the cha-cha-cha. My teacher thought it would be a good match; Frank could teach me sports, and I could show him how to glide around a dance floor.

One day, Frank noticed that Jerry seemed to be threatening me.

"Hey, Rob, what's going on with you and Jerry?"

"He's been asking me for money and things."

"Well, that's going to stop."

He went over to Jerry and turned him around.

"The next time you bother Rob, I'm gonna knock the shit out of you!"

Jerry knew he meant it. I was free! My pal, Frank, became my protector. But then came the sixth grade. Frank moved to California with his family. My heart sank.

"I see Frank left," Jerry taunted, "we're going back to the way things were."

I shuddered. To make matters worse, my sixth-grade teacher, Mrs. Millman, placed Jerry right next to me because he was a weaker student [dumb] and I was a stronger student. He cheated off me all year and my teacher didn't have a clue. I felt powerless.

Even one girl, Paula, bullied me. She was a bitch. Everyone hated her, both the 10-year-old girls and boys of Class 6-1 in Brooklyn's P.S. 215. Her cute looks and her perky nose, her blonde curls, and attractive dresses belied the truth. She was the evil witch from *The Wizard of Oz* and she always seemed to be scowling. Behind her back, we would sing the following ditty.

> On top of Old Smokey,
> All covered with grass,
> A bow and arrow
> In Pau-au-la's ass!

Nasty and spiteful, Paula took a strong dislike to our teacher, Mrs. Millman. In contrast, I had a crush on her and I often looked up her listing in the phone book and found that my beloved Mrs. Millman lived at 750 Ocean Avenue and her telephone number was Ingersoll 9-5259. One Saturday, I went into my parents' bed and hid under the covers hiding the phone. At 9:30, I put the call through.

Ring, Ring, Ring, Ring.

"Uh, hello…who…uh…is it?" Mrs. Millman inquired.

Oh no, I woke her from her sleep.

I got scared. Silence.

"Hello, hello… Who is it?" she was irritated now.

Click. I hung up.

She couldn't have known it was me. There was no caller I.D. in those days on black rotary phones and I knew from *Dragnet* she couldn't trace the call.

By Monday, I was sure she figured out that it was me who called. I was frantic and beside myself. The morning and afternoon passed, hour by hour, without a word. We went from math, to reading, to science without a hitch. By three p.m., I was relieved that I wasn't found out.

Paula had it in for Mrs. Millman. Who knew why? Was it because Mrs. Millman had real class, dressed beautifully, and had a smile that melted hearts? Did Paula want to be the queen and resented that she wasn't? Malicious and malevolent, Paula looked for every opportunity to undermine our teacher. She would convince kids to defy her instructions or answer her back disrespectfully. She would sit back and from the sidelines, let other kids do her dirty work. Kids were afraid of her, so they did her bidding. At the end of the school year, in a final coup, she tried to get us to not give Mrs. Millman a departing gift. We were graduating from sixth grade and going on to junior high in September. How could I not give her a gift? Many knuckled under. On the last day of school, there were very few gifts on Mrs. Millman's desk. I got her some perfume from the local pharmacy and a farewell card. Sadie gave me some money to make the purchase; she said it was only right. Mrs. Millman, visibly saddened by what seemed like a slap in the face, still managed to give me a smile as I gave her my present. I blushed.

Paula was not only a bitch; she was a *rich* bitch. I lived on the west side of McDonald Avenue where people mostly read the *Daily News,* hoping that the latest murder in the paper wasn't done by an Italian. Paula lived on the east side of McDonald Avenue where they read the *New York Times,* so they could peruse the business section for the latest stock exchange listings. They had money; we didn't. It was just how it was.

During the fall term, I mostly wore short-sleeved shirts. I owned one long-sleeved shirt; it was my favorite. It was an aqua color with a button-down collar. It looked great with a tie; we wore ties in those days. As December arrived, I was still wearing short-sleeved shirts and once a week my aqua, long-sleeved button-down shirt. One Tuesday, Paula seeing that I wore a lot of short-sleeved shirts, decided to get a rise out of me.

"You fruit!" she exclaimed as she looked askance at my shirt.

I looked her squarely in the eye and said, "You vegetable!"

We both laughed. I didn't know what she meant, but I knew it wasn't good.

December turned to January and January to February. One wintry day, I woke up and decided to wear my favorite shirt. I went to the closet and was horrified. My long-sleeved shirt was now a short-sleeved shirt!

Frenzied, I shouted out, "Ma, Ma! What happened to my shirt? Ma, Ma…"

"What's the matter, Rob?"

"Look at my shirt. It had long sleeves and now it doesn't. What happened?"

"Oh, honey, I saw that sleeves were frayed at the wrist, so I sheared them and sewed them back."

"Oh, Ma. *My favorite shirt.* Why didn't you ask me?"

"Oh, Rob, it really was frayed. I couldn't let you go to school like that."

I put on my new old favorite shirt and died a thousand deaths. Would Paula call me names again or would she just not notice? I only wanted winter to glide by bringing warmer weather. Spring finally came and Paula never said anything. As it turned out my father and hers did business together. They were both engineers. That seemed to cut the tension between us.

All through grade school, I didn't fully realize that my dad was starting a new business and money was scarce. During this time, he got sick and went to the hospital for three weeks; he had had a heart attack. It never occurred to me that the reason I didn't have a full array of long-sleeved shirts was because we couldn't afford it. We lived in an old house in a need of repairs, with a big yard. There was plenty of food on the table, lots of laughter, and family drama. Sadie and Frank shielded us from the reality of our financial straits. As time passed, it became apparent why we had so much pasta and why I could only give Mrs. Millman a card at Christmas, and why I kept on wearing hand-me-downs from my three older brothers. I learned that the reason we had the house was because my grandmother laid out the cash and lived with us.

A few years later, business picked up and my closet became replete with long-sleeved shirts. My wardrobe doubled when I became a teenager because my brother, Ron, and I shared shirts; he was five years older. I had a new favorite shirt: the pale purple one with the curl collar looked great with a black slim Jim tie. It drew raves from the junior high crowd. Since I didn't have to, I never wore a short-sleeved shirt in winter again. Sadie and Frank made sure of that.

I didn't know how to fight, but I knew how to pray. I relied on God whom I desperately needed to intercede on my behalf. Eventually, I learned that God helps those who help themselves. In junior high in 1954, I was in 7-1 and Jerry was in 7-15; the less academic kids were in the later numbers. At David A. Boody Junior High, our paths would rarely cross.

I was taller, older, and felt my former feistiness. Jerry came up to me and started badgering me.

"Give me some money!"

"Fuck you!" I retorted. "We're not back in elementary school. Those days are over. Just stay away from me. And, if you want money, get a fuckin' job!"

Then there was Joey.

"Hey, faggot! Where the fuck are you going?"

This went on for a short while.

"Hey, my faggot is here!"

I grabbed him by his shirt and threw him to the ground, hitting a wrought iron fence. He looked shocked, sprawled out on the sidewalk.

Trembling, I yelled out, "Eat shit and die, you fuckin' asshole."

That was the end of that.

Then there was Vinny. I'd pass by his house on the way to confession every Saturday afternoon. He was on his stoop.

"Hey, *Mary*, where ya goin'?"

"Go to hell," I retorted.

"Okay, Mary, I'll go to hell."

Then I became friendly with Johnny, Vinny's older cousin. He was handsome, tough, and he liked me. I remember every Friday in my second period math class, I would write my algebraic solutions on the sideboard, the *same* board every week. Every Friday, Johnny had a third period class in the same room. On top, I would write my name, hoping that Johnny would see it and know I was there the period before.

In the hall, "Hey, Bob, every week I see your name on the board, *Bob Scherma*."

"Oh, really?" I was in love.

One day, we got to talking about his cousin.

"Is my cousin giving you shit?"

"Well, maybe…"

"It won't happen again. You're a great guy."

My loins were on fire.

"Hey, Johnny, thanks."

I just wanted to make out with him and run my fingers through his curly locks.

Vinny was no longer a problem. I joined the football team at Lafayette High and when I played varsity, Vinny, a year younger, became our fullback. He started out as a "new boy" and revered my varsity status as a new boy usually did. It was amazing. My enemy became my admirer. How circumstances and people change. And I thanked God for that.

Chapter Five

A Priest Gives 'The Talk'

I knew I was attracted to men when I was four because I was turned on by the comic strip, The Phantom. On Sundays in the Journal-American, it was in color! He wore purple tights, a black facemask, and tight, tight black trunks. I *liked* him.

All through grade school and junior high, I had crushes on classmates and many of them were boys. And some of them were girls. It's not that I wanted to do anything with any of them, especially since I didn't know what I could do with them. I just wanted to be around them.

I was also a fervent Catholic.

One day, in Brooklyn, after a game of stoopball, when I was eleven, my friend, Rudy, asked me an odd question.

"Do you know about jerking off?"

"What's jerking off?"

"You don't *know* about jerking off?"

"No, what is it?"

He said, "Come in into the garage. I'll show you."

I said, "Sure."

We went through the alleyway to his backyard and into the empty garage. His mother and grandmother were off somewhere in the family Mercury convertible. No one was home.

Rudy closed the garage doors and pulled out his dick. It looked like a tree stump, thick at the bottom, and narrower at the top.

He said, "This is what you do," and proceeded to rub his dick, which got harder and bigger. After a minute or two, this white stuff burst out. By now, he was panting and moaning. He put his dick back in his jeans.

"So, that's jerking off," I said.

"You should try it," Rudy instructed.

Rushing out of the garage, I said, "You bet!"

And try it out I did.

By age twelve, I had been jerking off practically every day for over a year. Then I went to Catechism class.

They let us out of Boody Junior High at two p.m. on Wednesdays and we went over to St. Simon and Jude Parish for religious instruction. Father Haggerty gathered us boys in the school basement. The girls went with Sister Rose Agnes. This was unusual because our classes were always coed.

"Boys, today we have a very special topic. Does anyone know what *sex* is?"

We were stunned. Not a one of us answered. We all looked down. Sex? *Sex*? How could a priest talk about this?

"Well, you know, boys, that marriage is a holy sacrament of the Church and that God has designed a sacred plan to make children within the confines of Holy Matrimony. That is done through sex."

Help us, dear Lord.

"A man's penis gets hard; that's called an erection."

An erection! *O my god*!

"The man places his erection between a woman's legs into her vagina."

Vagina! Stop, please *stop*.

"In so doing, he plants his semen, a white, gooey substance that comes out of the penis, in her. If the semen penetrates an egg cell, which is in the woman, a baby starts growing."

Holy shit! That white gooey stuff! Penetrates an egg cell! Tell me he isn't saying all this.

"Now, boys, I have to let you know that having sex before marriage is a grave sin. Even thinking about sex and taking pleasure from the thought is a mortal sin. You will go straight to hell if you have any sex before marriage or take pleasure from impure thoughts."

This is terrible. Fire? Eternal damnation? I thought you could only go to hell if you missed mass on Sunday or ate meat on Fridays.

Father continued, "Now, there's something else. If you get an erection and rub your member up and down and ejaculate and waste your semen, it's a *mortal sin*! This is called masturbation. It is also called Onanism. God struck down Onan, in the Old Testament, because he wasted his semen. And know this, scientific studies have proven that you will wear out your *fibers* if you masturbate."

Mary, Mother of God and all you Holy Saints! Rub my member up and down! Wear out my *fibers*? I certainly didn't want to wear out my fibers; I knew I must really need my fibers, even though I had no idea what the hell they were.

Well, I went home and told all my friends that what we've been doing alone in bathrooms or in circle-jerks is a sin. *A mortal sin.*

Life was never the same after that. Now when I jerked off, I had to go to confession.

"Please, Mother of Purity," I prayed, "Keep me pure."

My first battle was not to masturbate. Then came the eventual submitting to sexual desire and finally, the subsequent guilt. What guilt! It was only Monday and I was hell-bent. Confession was Saturday and already I was *heartily sorry for having offended Thee.*

By Tuesday, I was horny again. I missed my bus stop because I had an erection and couldn't stand up. When I finally got home, I gave in. Again.

By Saturday, I had racked up a score of 10. If I had one mortal sin, what did it matter if I had ten? What the hell.

Now, most of what turned me on was men. We didn't have porn back then, but we had muscle magazines. I was attracted to men but was growing up in tough, Italian Brooklyn and was supposed to like girls. And, I wanted to like girls. But I wasn't driven to. I wanted to one day get married, have kids, grandkids, the whole kit and caboodle. But I liked men like Johnny Columbo down the block, who was older and in summer, wore his short sleeve shirt opened, so you could see his chiseled chest and his large, sterling silver crucifix. Yeah, I liked men. And I was a Catholic.

I soon found out that guys who liked guys were not liked. We were *faggots. Worse than being a girl.* A fag. I didn't want to be so reviled and I certainly didn't want to go to hell. I wanted to get married. Be normal. Be like my three older brothers.

I turned to prayer.

"God, make me like everyone else. *Please.*"

God was whispering something to me, but I couldn't quite hear Him.

Chapter Six

Vocation

I had to keep my inner sexual proclivities to myself, a secret. I had to make believe I liked girls when I liked guys. I was called a "faggot" and "Mary" for a reason. I was different from other boys. More like a girl. How, in God's name, could I reconcile my crushes on men with *Him*? I needed to be somewhere where *Someone* understood. I needed to know what Love was. I was in pain and in conflict. I needed to confer with my eternal friend. So, I went to church.

I went to confession to Father Scanlon. He was a ruddy-faced priest who came from Ireland. He'd be out shoveling snow or fixing a car or even playing softball with the kids. He smiled readily and made you feel like you were all right, no matter what you had done.

I began, "Bless me, Father, for I have sinned. It has been one week since my last confession."

"God bless you, son. Now, tell me your sins."

"Father, I masturbated three times. I had impure thoughts ten times. I lied once. I got angry two times. For these and all my sins, I am heartily sorry."

Sensing that I was being distracted from God, he gave me an unusual penance. Usually it was ten Hail Marys and ten Our Fathers.

He said, "I want you to go to the statue of the Sacred Heart and say ten times, 'Jesus, teach me to love you.'"

I paused for a moment and said, "Yes, Father, I will."

"God bless you, son. *Ego te absolvo…"*

At the same time, I began the Act of Contrition, "O my God, I am heartily sorry for having offended Thee…"

Afterwards, Father then said, "Go in peace. Your sins are forgiven."

What a peaceful feeling. The guilt I was carrying around had been wiped away. I was faultless and I was back in God's good graces.

Asperges me, Domine, hyssop, et mundabor. Lavabis me, et super nivem dealbabor.

[Cleanse me, O Lord, with the hyssop branch, and I shall be made clean. Wash me, and I shall be made whiter than snow.]

I walked over to the altar, genuflected in front of the Blessed Sacrament in the tabernacle, walked over to the statue of the Sacred Heart of Jesus, and knelt. The eyes on this statue were piercing. They gave the illusion that Jesus could look right into your heart, your soul.

I began, slowly, deliberately,

"Jesus…teach…me…to…love…you…. Jesus… teach…me…to… love…you… Jesus…"

I was a young man, maybe thirteen or so. This gentle soul asked me to ask *Son of the God who was Love* how to love Him. How wondrous this Father Scanlon was! His simplicity of faith touched me, deeply. He knew that I needed to speak directly to the Source of Love to learn how to love and how to love Him. I marveled at the sweet God Who sent me this wonderful priest.

At Lafayette High School, I joined the football team. I got a crew cut, wore a red parka, black chinos with a back buckle, a white sweatshirt, and U.S. Keds tennis sneakers, It was 1957. I started introducing myself as *Bob*. It was an amalgamation of James Dean and West Side Story, the two icons of the times. In Brooklyn, to be a man, you had to be into sports, you had to be tough. Football could satisfy those two criteria. Now, I wasn't tough and I wasn't a natural athlete, but the coaches said they would toughen us and teach us everything we needed to know to be a football hero.

It was a scary thing. What did I know about football? I tossed one around all of ninth grade on my block and dreamed one day I'd join this team. I started high school that September at the age of fourteen and was a "new boy" the very first week. New boys were considered the lowest of the low. We were exercised to death and did the bidding of the older members of the team. We worked out every day and on Saturdays, we would attend each game in the stands. We weren't given uniforms until we proved ourselves a full year later.

There were strict rules. No going out with girls. No being out after dark. Strict diet. No smoking. We had to maintain passing grades. Practice was brutal and was after class each day until after dark. Football was our life and because it demanded such a commitment, many guys dropped out. They were called *quitters* and you might as well hang it up rather than be called a quitter for the rest of your life. I knew I would never quit. Even if it killed me.

As each class went by, that nervous feeling in my stomach built up until we were finally out on the field. My football friends and I talked about it and commiserated and determined never to drop out. Our coach was a former marine, an all-city right end, and a total inspiration. Coach Sam Rutigliano would eventually become defensive head coach for the Cleveland Browns, but with us, he was a master psychologist. He knew how to handle each kid; one kid needed to be harassed to get the most out of him; but with me he knew to be gentle and inspiring. I was always appreciative of his encouraging words. He left before my varsity year and a less charismatic and less sensitive Coach Ken replaced him. We missed Sam very much.

While on the team for three years, I knew I was attracted to some of the guys, but not many. Who had energy for sexual excitement? Our coaches exhausted us. However, I do remember this one guy who gave other team members massages. He gave me one and I turned hard. What to do? I stayed on the massage table face down and just slept it off or pretended to.

I remember one team member, Gus, who seemed to fuck a different girl every night. He was a Beau Brummel and spent all his cash on sweaters. He had thirty-five of them! I was turned on to him but ignored it. I was totally intimidated by his prowess. Who could compete with him even though he was committing mortal sin after mortal sin? Still, I wondered what it was like to be him.

At Lafayette High School, while you were on a team, you were excused from gym to my delight. It was now my last term in high school and I had to go back to gym class for the spring semester of 1960. I asked Coach Ken if there was any way I could be excused from gym. He said, "Sure, Bob. You can watch the equipment in the football room. You're the only one I would trust there."

The room was long and narrow, and there was a gated area, which could only be entered into with a key. The really expensive football equipment was kept there. Coach gave me the key and I stayed there each day, second period from February through June, alone. I started to pray the rosary and became a more fervent Catholic. Being on the football team was a passionate and all-consuming experience. In the fall of 1959, we played our last game on the second Saturday of November. It was like being on a speeding roller coaster and suddenly stopping. I felt off balance, light-headed, and depleted of energy. Boredom seeped in and I slept a lot, a two-hour nap every day. I had dedicated myself to football, but now that was over. If I wasn't a football player, what was I? I asked God to lead the way. I certainly didn't know where to go or what to do. I didn't know who I was anymore.

In September 1960, I started Brooklyn College. I didn't make day school, The College of Arts and Sciences, and I didn't want to go to a Community College. I chose Brooklyn College's School of General Studies, night school. It was a blow to me not to be with my friends in day school at Brooklyn College. I knew I didn't study well during my football years because I was too exhausted; that didn't make me feel any better. I needed to get an 85-overall average to get in. I only had an 83.7, a severe blow to my ego. I felt like a jerk, a loser, second-rate. If you went to day school, you had self-respect. I hated myself for not getting an 85 average. What was the point of football? We ended with a losing season, the first in fifteen years at Lafayette High! What was all that about? I prayed for guidance and asked that I accept this as God's will.

I had mornings off. I started going to mass daily at 6:30 a.m. Soon I was staying for a second mass, for thanksgiving. I felt very calm and centered in my local church and I carried this peacefulness throughout the day. I heard a sermon once about vocations to the priesthood. I considered it and said to myself, "I could never do that. How could I speak in front of a congregation?" Yet, a persistent thought stayed with me and I pondered the words of Christ, "Leave everything and follow me."

During this first semester of college, I became very attracted to a young priest, Father Zeni. He was Italian, handsome, loved by the kids, adored by teens, revered by adults, especially the elderly. He was a priest's priest. I had a crush on him but didn't know what words to give this attraction. All I knew was that I wanted to be like him. I also knew I had sexual feelings for him. But this was not new to me. I remembered being in love with Johnny B. in the second grade and then his sister in third. I had crushes on guys and girls all the time, but mostly with guys. I remember having a crush on Henry in the seventh grade and Chris and Augi, the delivery boys from the dry cleaners, in the eighth. Of course, in high school, there was a succession of cute guys in tight jeans that I liked. I tried to ignore it, even went with convention and dated girls I liked. However, at this moment, I was in the middle of a crush with the man I was aspiring to emulate.

At Christmas high mass in 1960, Father Zeni was officiating. He gave a homily and spoke about young men being called to the priesthood and woe to parents who got in the way of this holy calling. The mass continued, the music swelled, and at Holy Communion, I dedicated myself to God and to the priesthood. I decided to follow Him and him at the tender age of seventeen.

I applied to the seminary of the Diocese of Brooklyn and Queens and entered the minor seminary in downtown Brooklyn near Eastern Parkway in September of 1961. During all this time, I struggled with my sexual feelings toward Father Zeni. I didn't want them, couldn't comprehend them, wished they'd go away. I prayed to God that they disappear, "Please stop these feelings." I prayed, but to no avail.

Being in the seminary meant being celibate. But to me, being celibate meant not only not having sex with others, but also not even having sex with myself. During Christmas vacation 1960, I vowed to be totally chaste, especially now that I was going to become a priest. No more sex. None.

At the end of June 1961, Father Zeni, after only two years as a priest, was given his own parish in another part of Brooklyn. I was devastated. How could I continue without my hero close at hand? Every time I felt his absence, which was every other moment, I prayed the Hail Mary; it became my mantra. I was tortured and couldn't abide his leaving. I prayed and prayed and prayed and finally was able to accept his departure and still wanted to be a priest. I saw Father Zeni as the vehicle for me to enter the priesthood. His role was over. Now it was just me. *God* and me.

Letters from Sadie could bring me back to earth. It was a Thursday afternoon at the major seminary in Huntington, Long Island. It was close to the Christmas holidays in 1963. Eddie Williams and I were hanging out in the auditorium. Eddie was playing piano and I was singing a song or two. Eddie and I were pals. He came from N.Y.U. and I from Brooklyn College and those of us who entered the seminary with public school educations bonded together. We were different from those guys who entered the minor seminary in freshman year of high school. We were from another galaxy. Catholic school guys put me a little on edge. They thought they were better than us. To further differentiate us, Eddie and I considered ourselves the resident Jews. We spoke with local New York Jewish inflection. At Passover, we made sure we brought contraband *matzohs* to our tables in the refectory. A little butter, a little salt: ah, heaven! H'ashem was proud of us.

It was one p.m., after dinner, we had gotten the mail and now we were on break doing music before our 3 p.m. class. I was reading a letter from Sadie and started to chuckle out loud.

Eddie, head up from the piano, asked, "What's so funny?"

"Oh, I got this letter from my mother in response to a letter I sent her last week. I asked her if I could bring the laundry home at Christmas."

Eddie, "And?"

"Well, I'll read it verbatim. Here goes, 'If you bring the laundry home, I'll break your balls!'"

Eddie, astonished, said, "No…"

I said, "Yeah…"

"Let me see that letter!"

I gave it to him. He laughed out loud.

I said, "You see why I have to save her soul… Do you understand what I'm dealing with here?"

Eddie smiled and nodded, "Yeah, I see what you're dealing with."

We picked out another song and then returned to our rooms before the next class.

And, yes, I sent my laundry out to our local Laundromat service before I went home. *You betcha.*

As God spoke wordlessly, there were many other voices in my head. There was one that said, "You belong here." And another that said, "Get out of here." Another voice asked, "Why am I falling in love with men?" I soon had a crush on the head Deacon, Bob. And then there was my next-door neighbor, Sean. He was the smartest in our class, cute and sexy, and I was definitely attracted to him but told myself it was nothing out of the ordinary. Everyone knew we were best friends and I loved my friend. There was a parapet outside our windows and he would climb outside on a moonlit, starry night and sit against the wall outside my window. I'd perch myself on the windowsill.

"Hey, Bob, look how gorgeous tonight is!"

"It certainly is gorgeous."

I was so happy to be there with him.

"I was talking with Iggy today and we concluded that it's the little things that count in life. The little things…"

"Like tonight. Simple beauty. Us enjoying all this."

"I'm glad our rooms are right next to each other so we can do this…even if you play the guitar in your room when I need to study."

I just wanted him to hear me, be with my music, and love it and me.

"I'll put a check on that, Sean. I'm just happy tonight."

"So am I."

We retreated to our rooms and I went to sleep feeling achingly content. My friend did love me and I loved him.

I started to read psychology books. Freud was the prevailing thought system in the books I came across and homosexuality was considered an arrested stage of development. He also explored the notion of bisexuality. Ah hah! That's what I was; a bisexual and I was stuck at an arrested stage of development. I figured it was a sexual immaturity and if that were the case, couldn't I mature sexually? Of course, I could. I could grow into a heterosexual, right?

Monsignor Coffey was the new rector of the Seminary. He was modern thinking, an intellectual, a product of the 1960s, very accessible, and manifestly compassionate. At the end of the first year in May 1964, we were having a spiritual retreat for three days that was psychologically oriented. I spoke with the retreat master, a priest, and told him that I wanted to see a psychotherapist, that I wanted to work out some issues. He asked me no questions and he gave me a name. At the end of the retreat, Monsignor Coffey called me to his conference room.

Monsignor looked elegant in his black cassock with red buttons. His face had the map of Ireland on it; milk-white skin, with eyes that seemed to pierce into you, and somewhat plump lips. It was a pleasant face and he had an agreeable demeanor.

He asked, "How was your first year here in the major seminary?"

I answered, "Fine, Monsignor."

"You know, I was reviewing the grades of first year students and I came upon yours."

"Yes, Monsignor?" I didn't like where this was going.

"You're not doing as well as you could. Is something bothering you?"

I hemmed and hawed and finally decided to tell him.

"Monsignor, I have a lot of things on my mind and I'm seeking help this summer. I asked the retreat-master for a psychotherapy referral and I'm setting up an appointment when I get home."

He smiled and his eyes beamed, "Great, we're on the same wavelength."

"Yes, Monsignor, we are," I said.

"I wish you good luck with your new venture," he said as he got up, "and I want to talk to you again in the fall when we return."

I said, "I'd love to, Monsignor."

I got up, he ushered me to the door, and I went outside for a walk. I was at peace. Help was on the way. And Monsignor was in my corner.

That summer I went to St. Mary's hospital on Dean Street in downtown Brooklyn and met with Dr. Rubio, a psychiatrist. He was from Peru and spoke with a Peruvian inflection. I saw him each Friday after my summer job. One summer afternoon in 1964, I entered Dr. Rubio's office with something on my mind. I smiled, sat down, and said hello. He was seated behind his desk as he smiled back and uttered his customary opening inquiry, "Mr. Scherma, what's new?"

"Well," I began, "I had this dream that's been bothering me. It was about Sean who lives next door to me in the seminary. We've become very close."

"Yes, I remember Sean; the valedictorian, the athlete, the musician. You're in a singing group with him and two others called *The Four of Us,* right?"

"Yeah, he's the one. He plays guitar and does a lot of the group arrangements. I'm the tenor. We have a Peter, Paul, and Mary sound. I've always been in choirs, even here in the seminary. I come from a musical family and love to sing."

"And, you had a dream..."

"Yes. Sean and I were taking a walk on a beach near the ocean. We were talking and walking and I was just so happy to be with him. And as we talked, I realized that I had sexual feelings toward him, and I woke up."

He asked, "How did you feel when you woke up?"

I answered, "Upset. Disturbed. I'm not supposed to have those feelings. I don't want to be a homosexual and these are homosexual feelings, aren't they?"

Dr. Rubio paused. Then he responded, "Don't be upset. Sean is *just a friend.* You have to see him that way. Those feelings are inconsequential. They're merely feelings. Sean is... just... a...friend," he said, drawing out the phrase.

"Just a friend," I repeated, wanting to believe it with my whole mind and soul, "Just...a...friend."

I left the office that day believing I could change my thinking and my point of view. Sean was just a friend and if I saw him that way, the sexual feelings would of course disappear. I resolved to work on this and do it with God's help.

"Jesus, teach me to love you."

"Mary, Mother of Purity, cleanse me of these sinful feelings."

When the summer ended, I told Dr. Rubio I would ask my rector if I could continue therapy in the fall after I returned to the Seminary. In September, I asked Monsignor if I could do so and he readily accepted the idea. He gave me permission to go to St. Mary's in Brooklyn every other Friday. And that is what I did. I didn't want people to know I was in therapy, except my close buddies who were sworn to secrecy. Fridays were free afternoons and it was easy to move about unnoticed by others. I'd hop a cab, take the L.I.R.R. to downtown Brooklyn and walk over to Dr. Rubio's office. After each session, I would meet my friend Ken for something to eat at Juniors.

One Friday afternoon, in October 1964, Dr. Rubio was talking about this lesbian couple that lived with a child of five or six. One of the lesbians dressed like a man in a suit, shirt, tie, and loafers. Dr. Rubio objected to her outerwear and said it would confuse the child. He pleaded with her to reconsider what she wore for the child's sake. To me, this woman was strange. I had never met a lesbian and was now presented with an image of a lesbian that I took to be the norm. I thought of my older brother Mickey's contemporary, our cousin Alfred. He was a hairdresser and was very effeminate. I heard he had gone to a psychiatrist who said he could never be changed and had to live with it. That was in the late 1950s. In relating this story to me, my Aunt Angie concluded, "He's to be pitied." I didn't want to be one of them and I certainly didn't want to be pitied. A man acting like a woman or a woman acting like a man, what could be worse?

I wondered about this lesbian mother who dressed like a man. What about her relationship with God? I thought about it and was troubled by it. How could she get to God? I decided to ask Monsignor Coffey.

We met and spoke for a while, but I couldn't bring up the overwhelming question I had about my own sexuality. Homosexuality in the seminary was anathema. Seminary staff was always warning us about exclusive, personal friendships. But I *could* ask about a lesbian I didn't know.

Finally, I said, "Monsignor, my therapist was talking about a lesbian and I had a question I wanted to pose to you. How does a lesbian get to God through the Church?" After all, since I was a kid, I was taught that there was no salvation outside the Church. I asked further, "Monsignor, what would you tell her?"

I awaited his answer.

He stopped for a long moment and thought deeply about his response it seemed to me. I sat there expectantly.

Clearing his throat, he spoke.

"I would tell her she would have to find God *outside* the Church."

I was taken by surprise, awestruck, speechless. I knew I had heard something that would affect my life for the rest of my life only I didn't know in what way or when. Did Monsignor have an unspoken understanding of my sexual conflicts in the face of finding God? Did he extrapolate from my story that I was really talking about myself?

I thanked Monsignor. I knew that he was talking from the writings of the German theologian Hans Kung who felt that there *was* salvation outside the Church. During the reign of Pope John XXIII an atmosphere of freer thinking was in vogue. Hans Kung was an exponent of that point of view and so was Monsignor Coffey.

"I would tell her to find God outside the Church."

*

The autumn months of 1964 went by and my psychotherapy became more self-revelatory. Dr. Rubio was pointing me in a newer direction. In clear terms, he told me what to do, "Flow with the stream, stop fighting the flow of life. Go with it." What that could only mean was that I should leave the seminary, go back to Brooklyn College, date women, and one day get married and have kids. It's what I desired. I just wanted to fit in and be like everyone else. I prayed and sat in silence and asked for Guidance.

One day, I woke up and it became perfectly clear to me. I had to leave. I saw it as a calling, a call to leave. As Joyce wrote in *Portrait of the Artist as a Young Man*, I saw it as a call "To live, to err, to fall, to triumph, to recreate life out of life." For me to be truly me, I had to go and create a newer self. I was six months away from a bachelor's degree in philosophy, but now that it was crystal clear that I had to leave. I decided to leave by the end of the semester in January 1965.

When my class entered the seminary, we were different than previous classes. We were recalcitrant and questioning. It was the early 60s, revolution was in the air and the old order was rapidly changing. In the Church, the Jesuits called this restless generation *The New Breed*. We questioned the *Summum Silentium*, which demanded silence after night prayers at 7:40 p.m. It had been so since the Middle Ages and we asked, "Why?" We were to keep silence during the day at appointed times and we thought the *Summum Silentium* absurd. We weren't allowed to read novels but we sneaked them in and read them after lights out. You could roll up a towel and place it on floor at the bottom of your door, close the bathroom, and barricade yourself in there and read even if lights were dimmed by 9:50 p.m. *Franny and Zooey* became my passion. We thought the rule was silly and irrelevant and we flaunted our disrespect for it. The staff didn't know what to do with our class.

I told Monsignor Coffey my decision to leave and he immediately got me in touch with Dean Kilcoyne at Brooklyn College. He was to be my contact person and would evaluate my records and place me on a matriculated path to graduation. He also gave me names of priests and other staff members at the Newman Center, the Roman Catholic organization on campus.

When I first told Monsignor, he asked me to not tell anyone. That was the House custom. The day you departed, you just left without saying a word. How could I do that to my friends? I started to tell my buddies one by one. We had a conspiracy of silence of our own. I wanted them to know and they were glad I told them. I would be there for another two months and we could adjust to my leaving during that time. Together.

I told my closest friends a week before I left because I found it most difficult to leave them. It was a mistake. I should have told them sooner.

The night before I left, a Saturday, people came up to me and kept on wishing me luck. Word had gotten out and now it seemed everyone knew. In the recreation room before night prayers, a spontaneous hootenanny broke out. There was song and laughter and a rousing good-bye. One by one, each wished me luck. I loved these guys and they meant a lot to me. I couldn't just leave and disappear and have people wonder what happened. It was not the way I did things.

And so, on Sunday morning after mass, I went to my room and all my close buddies, including Sean, came into my room and hugged me goodbye and wished me Godspeed.

Monsignor Coffey happened to pass by and saw the tumult. He entered my room and asked everyone to leave. He made a gesture with his hand indicating that I was a big mouth. He sat down on one of my chairs and spoke.

"Bob, I know this is a big move for you and I want you to know that I'll be praying for you. I have great faith in you and know you'll get a sense of calling soon. Rely on your faith in God. Let Him lead you. Give yourself to silence and listen."

"Yes, Monsignor."

"Well, I have to go to the refectory and you have to be going. I wish you the best of all good things. Be well."

"Goodbye, Monsignor." I said, "and thank you. For everything."

I couldn't find the words to let him know how much he meant to me. My eyes teared up. I hugged him and said goodbye. Another mentor had come and gone. The voice I needed to hear was his. I felt that God was speaking to me through him.

Monsignor left and I was alone in my room. I paused and thought long about the enormity of the moment.

I then put my jacket on, got my luggage, and while the House was at breakfast, I went out the front door and was greeted by my dad and my brother, Ted.

Ted said, "Rob, you drive home."

Ignoring my hesitancy, Ted said, "Here are the keys." He knew it was important for me to take charge.

I gathered my courage, sat behind the wheel of the family car, and started on the journey home. The seminary was behind me and a new path lay before me.

Chapter Seven

Going Home

For those who love with heart and soul,
there is no such thing as separation.
-Rumi

On this sunny, clear winter's day in January 1965, we left the seminary in Huntington, Long Island and headed home, toward the streets of Gravesend in Brooklyn. My oldest brother, Big Ted, sat up front with me as I drove the red 1960 Chevy Impala and my dad, Frank, sat in the back.

"Your mother is preparing a wonderful meal for you," Frank said.

"You mean pasta formaggio and sausage and meatballs and veal cutlets and salad and other goodies?" I asked.

"You bet. And the family will be there," Frank answered.

"Great, Dad." I smiled.

"So, Rob, what are your plans now that you've left the seminary?" Big Ted asked. Ted, my oldest brother, was very encouraging of me becoming a priest. I knew he was going to be supportive of my next move.

"Well, I'm going back to Brooklyn College and going to get a degree in math and become a high school teacher."

I was 21 and I figured by age 23, I'd be a teacher.

"Sounds like a plan. I think you'd be good at that. You're great with kids and you'd have fun," Ted said.

Out of all the age groups, teenagers were my favorite. I felt at home with them, and they trusted me.

I took the Southern State Parkway to the Belt and exited at Ocean Parkway and drove to Kings Highway. I went from the eastside to Van Sicklen Street near West 1st Street and made the turn. We were the fourth house on the left.

The *pink* one. Sadie loved pink in the late fifties and everything we owned was pink. We even had a pink '57 Chevy [they called it coral but it was pink enough for Sadie] that my brother Ron had totaled. I pulled into the driveway in front of the pink garage door, parked the car, got my luggage, and went into the house through the pink back door.

Sadie grabbed me with a big hug and a smile and said, "Welcome home, Robert! I'm so glad you're here. You know, I finally got used to the idea of you becoming a priest, and now you're not! You're driving me crazy."

"What else is new, Ma?"

I remembered five years back when I told Frank I wanted to be a priest. I worked at his loft at 424 Broome Street each Friday and at lunch in early January 1961, I told him the news.

"Robert, if that's what you want, that's what I want."

At the dinner table that night Frank couldn't contain himself. He blurted out, "Guess what, Sadie. Your son wants to become a priest!"

Startled, I said, "Dad! What the…"

At that moment, Sadie was transporting a serving bowl of pasta and broccoli to the table that she almost dropped midway.

Sadie at the height of melodrama shouted, "What! No, not my son! I don't want my son in a cage!"

My Italian American mother had little regard for religion and less for the Catholic Church. She wanted grandchildren from each of her four sons. No exceptions. She didn't like the idea of me not marrying.

"It's not normal," Sadie said. "Is that why you've been going to mass every day? I want you to stop!"

"Sadie, I'm not going to stop," I said quietly.

She didn't speak to me for a week. She slowly accepted the idea because it was clear there was nothing she could do or say to stop me. But she didn't like it. I applied to the minor seminary for the following September. It took her four long years to come around and now, I wasn't becoming a priest.

Alongside Sadie, there was Angie, my beloved Aunt, who still lived upstairs. She gave me a big hug and several kisses and welcomed me home, too.

Then Sadie said, "Go upstairs, Robert, and see Granny; she's been waiting for you."

Granny was very ill and going through the last stages of uterine cancer.

I went into the hallway and shouted out excitedly, "*Signora! Signora!* Where are you?"

I started to climb the stairs.

"I'ma here in the kitcha. Come upa, Roberto," Granny answered.

There she was, sitting regally at the kitchen table. Waiting. She tried to get up, but I saw that it was hard for her to do so.

"Stay, Granny, I'll come to you. How are you, sweetheart?"

She looked at me and started to cry.

I hugged her and now my eyes became moist.

"I'm home, Granny, I'm home."

"I didn't thinka I woulda see you again."

I knew she knew she was dying, and so did she.

"No, Granny, I'm here and you're here. And I love you."

She paused for a moment as I stood before her. She looked up at me and from her ancient body, her blue eyes fixed on mine. And then she spoke.

"Don'ta losa whata you got."

I was taken aback, stunned really. My first teacher of God spoke to the core of my soul and went right to the heart of the matter.

"Don't worry, Granny, I won't. I won't."

But I was worried. I was re-entering the secular world and feared I'd lose my faith, the thing I treasured the most. Outside the confines of the seminary, would I remain close to God? And if so, how?

After a while, Granny got tired. I helped her into her bedroom, where she lay down and rested.

"I'll see you later, Granny."

"*Buona*, Roberto, *buona*."

Her words trailed off as she succumbed to the respite that sleep gave her.

I went downstairs and saw that family was arriving; brothers, their wives, nieces, and nephews. It was wonderful to see everyone as we sat around the table for this welcome home feast.

At nightfall, everybody left and I went out to meet with some friends; Ken, Loretta, Rudy, the gang I knew from high school. I needed to see them, be with them, laugh with them, and talk with them.

On the following Tuesday, I went to Brooklyn College and registered for my next semester. I took two courses in the math curriculum, the two courses that followed the last courses I took four years back: *intermediate calculus* and *modern algebra*. I also enrolled in a teaching sequence. I started classes the following week. My new life was beginning.

That first semester back was arduous. I couldn't get my footing. I knew I was heading somewhere, but where? I couldn't concentrate or stay focused. Some days I felt so utterly alone and isolated as if afloat on a raft in vast, unknown waters. There were days I'd walk into a classroom, put my body into a seat, but my mind would be somewhere else. I thought the transition would be easier; it wasn't. I was now following a path of my own choosing and not adhering to a path laid out by others. I wasn't quite sure if what I was doing would work. Most of the time, I was anxious.

In mid-March, it was clear Granny was nearing the end. Her three children, Sadie, Angie, and Vincent were all there. We entered her bedroom one by one and talked with her, though she was apparently unconscious. We were all in the kitchen outside her bedroom when I felt a chill in the air. It was 7:30 p.m. I went inside to see Granny. She was gone.

I held her hand, which was still warm. I asked God to bring her home safely. I let go of her hand and stood by her bed. Alone. I noticed my hands were cold. I walked out of the bedroom and told Granny's children their mother was dead. They rushed into her room and saw for themselves. One by one, they came out and we hugged each other. I went downstairs and sat by myself. I recalled Granny and me praying together when I was a child in the very room I was sitting.

"Roberto, talka to the God anytima you wanna. He lova you."

But so did Granny and now she was gone. I sat there in silence.

"Don'ta losa whata you got."

A tear came to my eye.

With this loss, I couldn't feel God.

I felt bereft.

Chapter Eight

Somebody Up There Likes Me

The school term continued to unfold at Brooklyn College, and it didn't help that I took too much math too soon. I was falling behind. I had been away from math too long and by June, I had to change my major. *But to what*? I was now in college five years with no major in sight. I was tired of change and didn't know what to do. So, I went my counselor for the first time who looked over my entire record and saw that I was over-credited in Latin. He smiled at me and said, "Latin is your way out."

Latin? Latin? I needed only five more courses for this major to graduate the following June. Indeed, it was the only way out. So, I took The Elegiac poets, especially Catullus, who mourned his love for Lesbia, somebody's else's wife, the historian Livy, the orator Cicero whose eloquence was stunning, and Latin Prose Writing, a killer of a course. This is hardly what I planned, but I remembered the adage, "You want to make God laugh? Tell Him your plans."

From the time I left the seminary until now, I was troubled and painfully apprehensive. I pondered the words of Jesus:

"The Kingdom of heaven is like a mustard seed, which a man took and planted in his field. Though it is the smallest of all seeds, yet when it grows, it is the largest of garden plants and becomes a tree, so that the birds come and perch in its branches."

What would happen to the seeds of faith I had planted all these years? Would my faith die and wither away?

I believed that times of darkness pass into light and that bad times were followed by good times. Cicero in an essay on old age asked, "Didn't the happy times pass? So, too, the sad times." For me, now, pain had a function; it was to be for the sake of growth. Still, pain was pain and I was in the midst of hard times. With little vision, I made an act of faith in the future and believed it had to get better. Either that or sink into hopelessness. I expressed my pain to Professor Maxine Greene in an end term paper. Her personal handwritten response was most helpful at a moment I needed it most. [See Appendix 1]

It was now my last year in college. That summer, I took a psychology course, got an A, and wondered where psych had been all these years? However, I was now a Latin major and was preparing to student teach at Poly Prep, a school that future Ivy Leaguers went to. My professor was a former Latin teacher and scholar and I was his only student. He said I could have trained as a teacher in one of the few public high schools that offered Latin, but he thought Poly Prep would be a richer experience. He was right. Small classes, great mentors, and great kids.

As the term progressed, all I had to do was secure a Latin teaching job. I applied to agencies that placed teachers in Westchester, Long Island, and New Jersey. There were jobs, but I heard that there was a pregnant Latin teacher in Brooklyn's Fort Hamilton High and her name was Lola Caesar! She was to go on maternity leave in the fall and they needed a Latin teacher. I interviewed, the principal liked me, and said he would request me for the position. Of course, I had to graduate, take the licensing exam, pass it, and then he could get me on staff. I was thrilled. It seemed like a good school in a beautiful neighborhood and it had a view of the Verrazano Bridge!

At this time, the Vietnam War was raging. It was a long, expensive, and conflict-ridden war that pitted the communist government of North Vietnam against South Vietnam, with the U.S.A. as its principal ally. More than three million people were killed, including 58,000 Americans, and more than half of the dead were Vietnamese civilians. Opposition to the war bitterly divided Americans. I marched on Washington to stop the war and had a "Peace Now" sticker on the back window of my V.W. Beetle. The *love it or leave it* crowd didn't like us and considered us *commies*. We didn't like them and considered them fascists.

I wanted this teaching job at Fort Hamilton High, but there was only one problem, the draft. I was classified 1-A and that meant I could be drafted into the army right after graduation in June 1966 and carted off to Vietnam.

I had a thought. I telephoned my draft board on Surf Avenue in Coney Island and asked a question or two. Someone picked up the phone.

"Hello," a woman said.

I said, "Hi, I have a question. I was wondering if you could answer it."

"Sure, what is it?" She had a kind voice, not bureaucratic, sympathetic.

"I have a friend who's becoming a teacher and he's trying to secure a teaching job after graduation in June, but he's most likely going to get drafted because he's classified 1-A."

"Your friend," she inquired, "What does he need?"

"He needs more time. He won't get the job until mid-summer or so because of all the red tape at the Board of Education."

She asked, "What's he teaching?"

I said, "Latin."

"Latin? I took that in high school at St. Brendan's. How did he become a Latin teacher?"

"Well, he went to the seminary and left. He studied Latin there, went to Brooklyn College, and is now getting certified to teach it," I answered.

"Really? A Latin teacher in the public schools! Well, I'll be. However, honey, I don't think there's anything I can do, but tell your friend I wish him luck."

Despondent, I said, "Thanks, Miss."

I didn't know her name.

I got off the phone and figured my ass was going to Vietnam after graduation and goodbye teaching.

However, something happened.

A few days later, I got a notification from my draft board. Previously, I had been classified as a divinity student [4-D] and as a college student [2-S] and now available for unrestricted military service [1-A]. Those draft cards always came in the mail. I opened the envelope and here it was: a new draft card. I was reclassified 2-S; I had a student deferment. My God, this was my reprieve, my opening. It gave me enough time to graduate, take the exam, pass it, get the job at Fort Hamilton High, and start teaching in September. In that position,

I was classified 2-A and had a civilian job that was considered essential. Teaching was considered essential.

Apparently, that woman at the Draft board looked up records and deduced it was me. An angel was sent to me and her name was Marge Kennedy. An Irish lady, a Roman Catholic without a doubt, made it her business to find out who I was and gave me a student deferment. Her signature was on my new draft card.

All I could do was smile. I thought, *Somebody up there likes me.*

That summer of 1966 my ex-seminarian buddy, Paul, and I took a road trip to Cape Cod. Paul was a rotund, funny, loyal friend. He was another me. Not a sexual vibe in the least. I could pour my heart out to him and he could do the same with me. After leaving the seminary, we remained friends. Eventually, we both lived in the Village and would sometimes meet on a bench midway between our apartments on Charles Street and Seventh Avenue.

From the time I left the seminary, I saw that the Catholic Church wasn't doing it for me anymore. I went back to my old spiritual adviser, Father Villani, who was a loving and gentle presence. His words had no effect on me. What used to motivate me no longer did. I was uneasy and discontent and restless. I stopped going to mass and confession. What did I believe in now? I couldn't answer that question. I only knew that Catholicism didn't have the answers for me anymore. What I heard from the pulpit seemed trite and irrelevant. My relationship with God was, at best, tepid.

Paul and I were having a seafood dinner one night during our Cape Cod trip.

"I don't know, Paul, I'm having a hard time with the Church. I don't believe the way I used to."

"Yeah, I know what you mean. It's been hard since we left the seminary, but I still go to mass and do all the things I used to," Paul told me.

"I don't. I can't listen to all that anymore. Everything is a mortal sin. There's no room to think freely. I can't stand it anymore."

"To tell you the truth," Paul said, "I'm feeling a little disaffected myself. But I'm too scared to do or believe something different."

"Since we left, the world is a different place. Nothing makes sense. And another thing, what about sex? Are we going to wait till we're married? The way they want us to? What do they know? They're all celibates."

"Bob, you're heading into rough territory here."

"I know, I know. But something has to change. *Something*. I feel like I'm losing my faith."

Paul looked at me, speechless.

We finished our dinner with a cup of coffee and key lime pie. We were staying in a little bungalow colony, so we went back to our cottage into our separate beds and fell asleep.

About 2 a.m., I woke up and discovered I was horny as hell. I had a full erection. Nothing new. My young body wanted pleasure and relief, but I was still a Catholic and still remained chaste. I left my bed. I went outside and I looked to the starry sky. I prayed.

"God, I have something I want to say to You. I'm leaving the Church. It's over for me. I'm going out on my own and I want You to be with me. I'm not even sure where I'm going. But I'm willing to make mistakes and go down wrong paths, and even totally screw up. I need to find out the truth about myself and about You. Be with me as I go forth."

Two feelings overcame me. One was sadness that I was leaving what gave me such solace all these years. The other was exhilaration that I was embarking on the next stage of my journey. I recalled my conversation with Monsignor Coffey, "I would tell her she would have to *find God outside the Church.*"

I went to a shower stall that was outside this bungalow. I turned on the hot water and steamed up the room. For six years, I had had no sex with others or with myself. I slowly took off my clothes, entered the shower, and touched myself that night. That orgasm was a smoldering affirmation of my sensuality too long suppressed. I declared my new path.

From now on, *no rules* was *the* rule.

Chapter Nine

The Age of Free Love and Me

When I started teaching, I was twenty-three and some of my seniors were eighteen, even nineteen. The divide was narrow and oftentimes, I felt like I was one of them. I was green about life and still hadn't established an adult identity and certainly not a sexual one. I only knew I wanted to be straight, even if I was still attracted to men. I remembered Dr. Rubio advised me that my seminary love, Sean, was just a friend. It didn't matter that he invaded my dreams or that I was sexually attracted to him and that I couldn't get him out of my mind. Just friends. Subsequently, when I was attracted to some guy, I'd suppress and ignore it. Resolute and unwavering, I decided to look for a girlfriend.

For a couple of years, I dated women, seriously Catholic women who didn't want to have sexual intercourse. That was fine with me. I really didn't want to go to bed with them anyway. However, I liked making out, and touching, and being touched. But they and I were determined to *not* go all the way.

I soon became bored. I started to date some hot women who were already sleeping around; they scared me. Girls that really liked me couldn't figure me out. How come I wasn't making a move?

"You're a strange guy, Bob."

That always made me feel just great.

I went out with a teacher at my school, a "good" Irish-Catholic girl; her name was Meghan. People liked us together; we were a cute couple. We went out for a year and met the following summer of 1967 in Lausanne, Switzerland. We were on separate European trips. We spent one lovely, even magical evening together. We sat at an outdoor café sipping drinks. Her eyes sparkled and her smile was beguiling; I was mesmerized. I fell in love with her that night and was ready for more of a commitment. When we got back home weeks later at the start of a new term, I had a dream that she and I were married. I couldn't breathe and had to get outside or suffocate. I was having a panic attack. My commitment wavered and I was neither here nor there with her. She soon started dating someone else at school and afterwards, they became engaged. My ego was bruised but I knew I was kidding myself. I was in love with love and star-filled nights in romantic settings. Not the stuff of firm commitment.

It was the 1960s, a time of tumultuous upheaval when new cultural mores were established. Drugs, sex, and rock 'n roll. But I was a child of the 1950s; uptight, rigid, and conservative in attitude, especially concerning sexual matters. I was no longer a Catholic but still behaved like one. I was proof that you can take the boy out of the Church, but you can't take the Church out of the boy. Or as Sadie used to say, "He's still got the priest in him."

I decided I had to give sex a try. I was at a party uptown when I met Penny. She had short-cropped blonde hair, wore tight jeans on her slim body, and emanated a laid-back sexuality. Over a glass of Mateus, she told me she was working on the music for a children's show at her niece's school. I said I'd like to be involved. The following Monday, Penny came over to my apartment. We went through the storyline and selected scenes where songs could go. With my guitar, I wrote the music, and with pen and pad, she wrote the lyrics. After several songs were written and several glasses of *rosé* were consumed, we had our clothes off and before I knew what happened, I came. We didn't try again and I felt like a failure. Afterwards, she just wanted to be friends.

My friend, Sean, left the seminary in Innsbruck. He told me he had a romance with a charming girl who was a Mormon in Austria. They didn't have sex and eventually, they broke up. Sean then met Debbie in New York: she became the first woman he slept with.

I had several reactions. I was happy Sean moved back to New York. I had missed him being around for two years and wanted him nearby. Then I was jealous of Debbie. I couldn't exactly define why, but I was. I knew I would have to like her because Sean did. I also had to deal with the fact that though I tried to see him as a friend, he was more than that to me. I was in love with him and he just loved me. All right, I was his best friend, but still *just* a friend. And even if he turned out to be gay, I certainly didn't know what I would do. Anyway, it was out of the question.

I felt competitive. Sean had gotten laid and now, I wanted to catch up to him. I told him I was still a virgin that I had tried with Penny but came too fast. He laughed.

I was hurt by his response but didn't say anything.

In 1967, the Beatles were singing *Love, Love, Love. All you need is love.* Later that year, the classic Mike Nichols film, *The Graduate*, came out to much acclaim and notoriety. An older more experienced woman, the infamous, Mrs. Robinson, initiates a younger recent college grad into sexuality by seducing him. I determined to look for my Mrs. Robinson. I also determined to go back into therapy.

In 1970, I was out of the seminary five years and was still perplexed about my sexuality. My friend, Ken, was seeing a shrink and encouraged me to go.

I knew Ken since I was a kid from the old neighborhood. Ken was a nerd with a compassionate heart and a great sense of humor. We traveled cross-country twice. He and I were pals and we felt safe with each other as we talked about our lives year after year. I was not attracted to him sexually because he was overweight and my obsession with my own weight eliminated any attraction to overweight men or women. We became tight when we were teenagers attending Lafayette High School. He had a photographic memory, was a good listener, and we always had something to say to each other. We would walk a mile to Lafayette each day and talk up a storm. One day, we were walking through the Marboro Houses near the high school and we happened upon three teenage girls who were singing Happy Birthday to the girl with the sweet sixteen corsage.

"Happy Birthday to you! Happy Birthday to you! Happy Birthday dear JoAnn, Happy Birthday to you!"

They giggled and walked on their way to school.

Witnessing all this were two members of the Marboro Houses janitorial staff who were hoisting Old Glory up the flagpole. These quintessential Brooklyn types started to sing.

"Happy Boidday to ya pussy! Happy Boidday to ya pussy! Happy Boidday to ya pussy..."

Then the finale, "Happy Boidday to your *CUNT!*"

Shocked and horrified, Ken and I, innocent juniors, were totally scandalized, but not really. We laughed out loud. We didn't know how sexist this kind of scene was; it was commonplace in the 1950s and certainly in the Brooklyn we grew up in.

At age fifteen, Ken became a Catholic. I was his godfather for his confirmation. To this day, he addresses me as "Godfather" on special celebratory occasions. Ken wrote a poem commemorating that relationship. [See Appendix 4] We were seminarians at the same time in different places and left about a year apart. I was his best man for his first marriage. When that marriage went on the rocks, I delivered his divorce papers

I'd been in individual therapy, but Ken was now in both individual and group therapy. Before each group, he would visit me for an hour since his shrink's office was two blocks away. I'd make some tea and with cups in hand, seated on the couch, we'd chat.

"Twice a week?" I asked.

"Yep. In *group*, Jack sees you in action. In *individual*, you get to analyze your behaviors with him as well as what you can do differently."

He explained that Jack's therapeutic approach emphasized that feelings were unreliable when making life decisions. Relying on sound reasoning is the only remedy for neurotic functioning.

"We keep on doing the same thing over and over again hoping for another outcome. Never happens. Thinking is the way out," Ken said, parroting Jack.

As I listened, I was thoroughly fascinated. I also knew it scared the shit out of me. I had never been in group before. I might not like what I found out.

One day, I asked Ken for Jack's number. But I didn't call.

Ken kept visiting me week after week before group and after six months of carrying Jack's number around, I finally called him. I made an appointment for the following Monday.

I rang the street doorbell of a turn of the century building on West Eleventh Street and climbed to the fifth floor and entered a modest two-bedroom apartment. Jack smiled warmly, and asked me to come in. He was unremarkable looking, medium height and weight with a crew cut and wearing a generic white shirt and dark slacks. He looked very ordinary but had a kind manner and was soft-spoken and inviting. I liked him.

We walked through a larger room that was strewn with couches and chairs to the back room with a desk and two comfortable chairs. Jack sat down and asked me to do the same.

Then he asked me what brought me to his office. I told him I'd been talking with Ken and decided after a while that I wanted to get back in therapy.

"What do you think you'd like to work on?" Jack asked with what seemed like a neutral look that belied his concern.

"Well, I was in the seminary and I kept on having homosexual crushes, which I've had all my life since I was a kid. I was in therapy and tried to work this out. However, I keep on going out with women and I don't have sex. I think it's time I have sex."

"I suggest that you *not* take your homosexual feelings seriously. They're part of the furniture like a chair; it's there, just don't sit on it."

Well, I agreed. This was precisely my agenda; to get married like my three older brothers and have kids. Jack and I were aligned.

"We don't look at the past. I feel it's not what brings results. We start with the *now*, and figure out what to change now so that you can have a more productive future," he said. I was game.

It was different from the therapy I did with Dr. Rubio. This sounded more cerebral and certainly not psychoanalytical or insight oriented.

"I'll see you next Monday, Jack."

After three or four Mondays, on a Thursday in June, I started group.

I was the first one to arrive and Jack was in the back room with a patient. I took off my raincoat, hung it up, and sat down. I picked up a Newsweek magazine and perused it barely seeing the print, I was so nervous. A few minutes later, people started trickling in.

A pretty young woman said, "Hi, my name is Judy."

"Hi, Judy. My name is Bob. Are you new to Jack's group?"

"No, I've known him for about a year. I'm coming from another group."

"This is my first group with Jack." Then I asked, "What kind of work do you do?"

"I teach literature in college."

For a moment, I felt a little intimidated.

"I teach Latin in Brooklyn at Fort Hamilton High."

"That sounds interesting," she smiled. I felt a little more comfortable.

Then Jim came in. He had a beard, wore a red jacket, a plaid shirt and jeans. I introduced myself and after greeting both Judy and me, he started talking to Judy about a film project. They apparently knew each other outside of group.

I asked him if he was a filmmaker and he told me he was working on an independent film about homeless youth. I was intrigued and a little anxious. I'd never met a filmmaker before.

Others filed in and soon Jack appeared and the group was ready to begin. It was clear I was the new kid on the block. Everyone knew each other, except me.

Jack asked, "Who would like to work?"

Jim spoke up, "I'd like to talk about a woman I'm seeing. The *cunt's* name is Mary."

Jack asked, deadpan, "What's the rest of her called?"

The group roared.

Undeterred Jim continued, "She's driving me nuts. I don't know why I keep on seeing her. She's sleeping around and I get to see her in between. I want to see just her. She wants to see others."

Jack, "What makes you stay?"

"The sex is good and I like her."

"It looks like she's in charge and you have no power. Is there another way of looking at this? You're emphasizing your *feelings*. What do you *think*?"

"I think I should go look elsewhere if I want a monogamous relationship."

"Let your thoughts guide you. They're more reliable than your feelings," Jack said.

"I know what I *should* do, but will I?"

Peter spoke out loud, "At least you have a woman and you're having sex."

"Go ahead, Peter," Jack said.

"I'm incredibly lonely and depressed. My sex life is terrible; it's come to a screeching halt."

I froze on the spot and thought, *A poor sex life is better than no sex life.*

I sat there quietly as Peter droned on about his sad life.

Diane, good looking and polished in appearance, seemed to be simmering and snapped, "Stop wallowing in self-pity! You're so annoying. If you don't like your life, Goddamnit, do something about it. Just stop moaning and groaning."

Peter was taken aback, "I, I…"

I chimed in for him, "Maybe Peter needs some time to regroup before he can take the next step."

"You don't have to speak for me. I'll speak for myself," he snapped at me.

I thought, *Fuck you, asshole.*

I now noticed that his appearance was uncoordinated and the fact that he needed a bath irritated me all the more.

Diane said, "Just stop feeling sorry for yourself. Get a goddamned grip."

Then Jeff said he'd like to work.

"I'm having relationship problems in the collective I'm living in. People don't like me."

"What do you mean?" Jack asked.

"Well, I tend to be sloppy and don't wash dishes and don't like to do other house chores. People are always getting on my case."

I asked Jeff, "What's a collective like? How does it work?"

Bill interrupted, "Why are you asking about his *collective*?"

I said I wanted a point of information. Bill had caught on that I was threatened by the concept of a collective. He was right and I wanted to smash his face in.

"You know, Bill, what are you the *second* shrink? Jack is perched on one side of the couch, with you on the other. You remind me of bookends," Jeff said.

Diane, speaking to me, chimed in, "And you're in the middle!"

The group cracked up.

"This is bullshit!" Barbara yelled out. Barbara was a brassy broad, a blues singer who travelled cross-country on freight trains to develop her "machismo" as she'd revealed in earlier remarks.

"I think this group is too green for me! I've been in therapy too long and I want to finish soon. I don't think I can learn anything from you guys. Just callin' it as I see it."

I identified with Barbara on two counts. First, as a musician since I played the guitar and had composed about ten songs. Second, because I needed to develop my machismo too and take more risks. I gathered up my courage and spoke.

"I think it's absurd that you can't learn from me," I said. "How do you know what I know couldn't be helpful to you? Give us a chance, Barbara, give us a chance."

She melted. I was delighted.

"Maybe you're right. I'm just upset tonight and I'm impatient. I'll stay here in this group. I didn't mean to insult anyone."

Then Erica, a wisecracking, Jewish, hippie type from the Upper West Side spoke up, "Barbara, I'm not insulted and I'm glad you're staying in the group. I have something I want to bring up."

"Go ahead, Erica," Jack said.

"I'm going with Anthony who's a member of the Mental Patients Liberation Front. They fight for mental patients' rights. I want to go down to Cuba with the Venceremos Brigade and cut sugar cane for the revolution. Anthony doesn't want me to go. What do I do?"

"What do you think you'd like to do, Erica? Anthony is *not* your father" Jack inserted.

"I think I want to go because I believe in what Fidel is doing," Erica said.

I thought, *Holy shit! A communist in our midst! And no one is upset about it but me.*

I was an uptight conservative Catholic, trembling, *naïve*, almost without a clue. Though I lived in the Village, I was still a Brooklyn boy at heart; an Italian American kid who grew up in a neighborhood where the guidelines were clear. Everyone thought the same, everyone was the same, and everyone knew what was expected; get a job, get married, have kids, put them in Little League, and live in the old neighborhood. Now I was in *New York City* where *no one* was the same. I had no idea what to do; but I knew this group was a step out of Brooklyn into another country. I sallied forth, cautiously.

It was now 1971 and after a year of therapy with Jack, he moved to San Francisco and many of his patients followed him. It seemed almost cult-like to me. I stayed in New York but traveled there summers to visit Ken who relocated to Berkeley and Erica who moved to San Francisco. I toyed with the idea of going to the California School of Professional Psychology but didn't enroll because they weren't certified.

Before Jack left, he suggested I go to Group Labs, a gestalt group on the Upper West Side, where *feelings* reigned supreme. He thought it would be a good balance with his work. One day, my new therapist at Group Labs, Frayda, addressed me directly. She was a straight-shooting New Yorker and in a gentle way told you exactly what she was thinking. Her great big smile always disarmed me.

"Bob, you keep on telling us in group that you are turned on by men, right?"

"Yeah, but I don't want to be gay. I just have to live with it. I want to get married, have kids, the whole package," I responded.

"I understand, Bob. You want to fit in. But I have to tell you something."

"What, Frayda?"

"You've always had those gay feelings and you always will. If you don't accept them, you'll always be denying a part of yourself. Always."

I said, "But…" and kept quiet.

I let that sink in and placed it on the back burner to simmer. Both, Jack and Dr. Rubio, wanted me to ignore my attraction to men and be straight. Now Frayda was suggesting another way, the gay way. It didn't seem possible or probable. I just couldn't. I just *wouldn't.*

I needed to fit in; it was uppermost in my mind. I just wanted to meet a woman, fall in love, get married, and have kids. Jack and Dr. Rubio won the day. I was determined to be straight all the way. So, I decided to meet women and get on with it.

Chapter Ten

The Women in My Life

Jayne

Jayne was a teacher on staff and I was attracted to her. She wore tight-enough skirts and high-heeled stilettos. Her short, brunette hair was pushed back, so you could see her laughing brown eyes as she surveyed you, making an assessment she wasn't disclosing. Her lips let you know a wisecrack was coming. She and I both had a share at a ski house in Vermont. One evening in April 1970, I started a conversation when we were alone. We were sitting on a sofa, sipping wine.

"Jayne, I'd like to talk to you about something. Do you mind?"

"Why, no. What's up?"

"This is hard for me."

"What's the matter, Bobby? Maybe just say it. It's okay," Jayne reassured me.

"Well, it is embarrassing. Okay, here goes." And then quickly, "I've never really had sexual intercourse before." I was twenty-seven.

"Okay…" Jayne was thirty-one.

"I was wondering, you know, since we like each other… Do you think you could…teach me?"

"Well, Bobby," she paused and then said, "Let me just think about it. It's possible, but let me just think about it."

"Sure. Sure. Let's go slowly," I said as the door to the living room swung open and some of the others came in from the night.

The next day we were alone and chilly and so we got comforters and made a bed on the floor. With our clothes on, we started touching each other and continued even as people came in from skiing. I liked it and when we returned to the city, we continued to fool around like that for a while. Touching each other.

When it became clear that we would go to bed, Jayne said, "Bobby, I need to get back on the pill and when that kicks in, we'll play."

"Great, Jayne!" I was getting more excited by the idea.

One Saturday in June, we went to a barbecue in Nassau County at some school friend's home. It was a glorious day and people just had a wonderful time and Jayne and I loved spending time with them and with each other. At nightfall, we drove back into the city and went to my place on West 13th Street. We started to make out, and soon our clothes were on the floor. She tried to guide my erection but I got too excited and came before I entered her.

Exasperated, I looked at her and said, "It's either feast or famine."

Jayne smiled in her easygoing way and said, "Let's wait a while and we'll try again."

"Okay... We'll try again." I never thought of that. Try again, of course. What did I know? My Mrs. Robinson knew. After all, when the student is ready, the teacher appears.

We had some wine, chatted warmly, lit a few candles, put on the stereo, and soon we were at it again. Success! It was fabulous! I liked it so much we did it again and then again in the morning. I just smiled and smiled and smiled,

I drove Jayne home that summer morning in June 1970 and looked forward to spending a summer making love. And we did just that. One night I came five times and thought, *I am definitely making up for lost time.* But I was still conflicted about my relationship with God. After taking Jayne home after our first lovemaking, I went to Brighton Beach and carved a question in the sand, "Where are you, Jesus?" I couldn't find him, hear him, *feel* his presence like I once did. But like *Siddhartha*, I continued on my path. and put one foot in front of the other.

Jayne and I were just good friends having sex; we weren't in love with each other. As a matter of fact, she was longing for some medical student in Canada. He was keeping her at arms' length. In her mind, our affair was giving her leverage with this guy while I was learning the art of making love. We both were getting what we wanted.

Jayne decided to pursue her medical student and told me our time together was messing with her head. Eventually, she moved to Canada to see if she could marry him. Our run was over; it had its beginning, middle, and end. It was complete. We stayed friends until she left. It was now time for me to find someone else.

*

Ana

In 1972, my cousin Robert got married and I was his best man. In the wedding party, there was a beautiful Hispanic girl, Ana, whom I was attracted to. I struck up a conversation with her at the reception and eventually asked her out. She was pretty, intelligent, and was training to become a psychologist at N.Y.U. Her father was from Andalucía in Spain where he still resided. A sculptor and an intellectual, he was also was a communist who hated the fascist dictator Franco. Her background made her very interesting to me.

After a few dates, we went to bed. I was fearful that I wouldn't be able to perform, but there was no problem. Sex was good at my end, but Ana had trouble with orgasms. At that time in her life, she just couldn't totally let go. But she was exotic, and fun, and so presentable. Sadie loved her. Frank loved her. Everyone loved her. Little by little, I fell more and more in love with her.

During the early stages of my dating Ana, I met another woman, Amelia. She was Puerto Rican, a graduate of Barnard College, and worked at W.B.A.I., a left-of-left F.M. radio station in New York City. We were both in Group Labs where anger was deified. She told me she would be traveling in California that summer; I told her so was I and that I'd be staying with Ken and his girlfriend. We met one August afternoon in Berkeley and decided to go to bed. I had an erection and then lost it.

She started yelling at me, "You show me this magnificent instrument and then you take it away. You withholding bastard."

I retorted, "Fuck you! Do you think this is fun? What, am I doing this on purpose? You think you've got problems? I've got my own. Go to fucking hell!"

She looked at me. I looked at her. We started kissing and passion took over. Anger cleared the air.

As time passed, we discovered we *always* had orgasms simultaneously. She would say, "We…are…*stars*," and stars we were.

One time, she informed me, "My gynecologist told me I had *a classic cunt*."

87

I quite agreed with her doctor but couldn't help but laugh out loud at her declaration.

I loved this time of my life. You know how a song recalls a time vividly?

"Me and Mrs. Jones… We got a thing goin' on…" does that for me. It was 1972-73 when I went out with both these women at the same time and did it openly. When one got on my nerves, I went to the other. And then when the other was busting my chops, I went back to the first.

One time, Ana picked up the phone at my apartment and it was Amelia.

"Hello, this is Ana. Who's this?"

"This is Amelia! Is Bob there?"

"Amelia! Yes. He's here. Bob, it's *Amelia!*"

I put my hand to my forehead and grabbed the phone, "Hi, Amelia, what's up?"

"I don't like her. She sounds smarmy. Anyway, I just wanted to say hello, but I see you're busy!" She spoke in clipped tones.

"I'll call you tomorrow," I whispered. Thank God, Ana had gone to the bathroom.

When Ana returned, I was off the phone and she said, "She sounds like *una bruja*! I don't like her."

I knew that *una bruja* was a witch, but I couldn't get the rest of what she said under her breath. I didn't understand Spanish, let alone Castilian Spanish. I knew it wasn't complimentary.

"Why don't we go out for a bite to eat?"

She grunted, "Okay," and we left the apartment and I just waited for this moment to pass. The elevator ride down to the ground floor seemed an eternity. We walked down West 13th Street and made a left turn onto Greenwich and sat down at the Village Den and ordered hamburgers and fries. The moment had passed as I sunk my teeth into a juicy cheeseburger with bacon. Afterwards, Ana had to go to the Bobst Library to study. I had to go back to the apartment to do some reports for work.

Months passed by and one day in January, after an afternoon of lovemaking, Amelia asked me a question I wasn't expecting.

"Is this relationship going to go anywhere else?"

Without thinking, I said, "No."

That "No" put the kibosh on our relationship. There was nothing more to say. She asked me to leave her apartment on Bleecker Street and that was that.

By this time, I was falling deeply in love with Ana. We moved in together into my West 13th Street apartment and I dreamed of marrying her and having kids with her.

We spoke about future career moves. Ana was on her way toward a doctorate in psych. I was now working with younger problem kids in Bay Ridge as a newly baptized guidance counselor.

"Bob, you have this new guidance job…" Ana said.

"I do. But sometimes the kids have severe problems that I don't quite understand and certainly don't know what to do about."

"I know you just finished your guidance degree, but I think at some point, you should get a degree in psych."

Ana planted a seed and I let it grow, slowly.

Living together in a studio apartment wasn't easy. I was working hard and came home tired and Ana was studying, studying, studying. There was no space for privacy and it wore us down. Ana was still not having orgasms and that created more tension between us. I didn't see it, but she was gradually moving out of our relationship. She was becoming more independent and wanted to be her own woman.

We spoke about breaking up. Ana told me that her therapist Carolyn asked her, "Do you really want to walk away from love? He really loves you."

Carolyn was on my side, but Ana wanted to get her own place at Washington Square Village and build her own life. I helped her move in and of course, there was one last bout of lovemaking. She had two orgasms! She could finally let go when she let *me* go.

We decided on a three-month moratorium. After that time, we met for lunch. I hoped against all odds that she'd want me back. However, she didn't. She loved her new life without me and I had to admit she looked happier. I went into a depression and stayed low.

My guidance job didn't get re-funded and I wound up working back at Fort Hamilton High, teaching psychology and philosophy as literature. I was also a student in a psych program at Queens College. I was distracted and still missed Ana very much. I missed her smile, her reassuring words, her understanding. I missed coming from behind her, embracing her while she washed the dishes, gently grabbing her breasts, and saying, "I love these little tits!"

It was a routine.

Then she would say, "They're not so little…" with a Spanish accent.

"You're right, Ana! They're *big* little tits!"

We'd laugh and I'd hug her close.

But there was no going back. It was done. I needed time to heal.

*

It's interesting. I was going out with two women. With one I had incredible sex, and the other not. I fall in love with the one who couldn't have orgasms. Madonna/whore dichotomy? Could I not allow the two to exist in one person? Was Catholicism too deeply embedded in my being? Or was I just being loyal to Sadie? Or was something else going on? I remember saying one day in therapy that I loved both Ana and Sean the same. How was I to make sense out of that?

During this time, I simply suppressed my homosexual feelings. I'd see a cute guy behind the counter at Balducci's and I'd just be aloof with him even as I got turned on. If I noticed a good-looking man as I walked down the street, I just didn't dwell on it. If I was attracted to Al Pacino in *Dog Day Afternoon*, I just ignored it. My Catholic training taught me how to compartmentalize feelings and unwanted thoughts. I knew how to keep away from *occasions of sin*.

What would it have been like if I married Ana and had kids and lived a "normal" life. I think I would have been distracted by the demands of marriage and fatherhood but would still be attracted to men. Maybe I'd see some handsome dad at the playground or some gorgeous guy at the gym. It would never stop. Knowing me and adhering to Shakespeare's maxim, "To thine own self be true," I would have done one of two things. I would have stayed with Ana and the kids and not acted on my gay feelings. Or I would have left the marriage and joined a gay father's group and learn how to be a dad who was gay. In so doing, I would have done irreparable harm to Ana and the kids and would have had to live with that guilt for the rest of my life. It would have been a more complicated trip, but I'd have kids and I'd love them.

Sadie was upset that Ana and I broke up. She implored, "Robert, don't bring anyone home anymore unless you're going to marry her." She missed Ana terribly.

After bemoaning the fact of our breakup, I decided enough was enough. I went for the familiar. I looked for another girlfriend. In fact, I prayed for one.

Sarah

Sarah was a drama teacher. Recently divorced, I remembered watching her work with her students in the school auditorium one afternoon. She was gorgeous. I realized I had a penchant for beautiful women, and I discovered they did for me, too. Maybe it was the contrast. My women were elegant and me, well, as my friend, Erica, described me once, "I looked like a dissolute Italian Count." The contrast of opposites worked once more. I asked her out.

Sarah had blue eyes, a Semitic look, and was very funny and bright. She was Jewish and I was Italian and the combination worked very well. We were a fun couple. The two of us were always "on" and people loved to be around us. She had a beautiful voice and a theatrical presence. We were together for two years.

One Friday evening at her place, Sarah brought out a brandy she discovered the previous summer in Greece.

"Hey, Bob, would you like some Metaxa? It's really good."

"Sure, I'd love some."

She poured two snifters and gave one to me.

"I remember first having some in Mykonos. I had a lot and started dancing on tables. Had a great time."

We clinked glasses and said, "Cheers."

"How smooth this is!" I remarked.

"I knew you'd like it."

We were sitting on the rug and I pulled over my guitar. I started strumming a few bars of *Here, There, and Everywhere*. She sang and I accompanied her with some harmonies. We sounded good together and went from one song to the next. It was a great combination; Sarah and me and Metaxa and music.

After many songs and several glasses of Metaxa, I glanced over and suggested, "Let's go to bed."

With a grin and a mischievous glint in her eye, she said, "Okay."

It was the era of Women's Lib and so discussions of who was going to be in charge of contraception were up for consideration. Seemed logical to me. So she would use a diaphragm and I would alternate with condoms. We never had sex without protection. One Saturday night in autumn 1976, Sarah and I had gone to a Laura Dean dance concert, got stoned, and came home horny.

She didn't have any spermicidal jelly in her apartment, and I didn't have any condoms. We said *fuck it* and made love anyway.

Weeks later Sarah didn't get her period; she was pregnant.

Now Sarah and I knew the unspoken truth about us as a couple. We were passing time until the real thing came along. We had a great time together, but we both knew we were basically incompatible. She was athletic and I wasn't. I liked to sit; she liked to move. She was an only child, and I was one of four and she resented my family. She wanted to marry someone from *the* tribe; I belonged to another one.

We had a decision to make. Sarah wanted an abortion. I didn't.

I said, "Sarah, have the baby and I'll raise it. I don't know how I'll do it, but I'll figure it out."

I didn't believe in abortion.

She said, "No, Bob, I can't have a baby at this time of my life. It's not like we planned it. I want an abortion."

Sarah said that with such resoluteness and since I believed that a woman had control over her own body, I agreed. Just like that.

She set up the procedure for a Friday in November. We both took off from work and the abortion was performed.

That night we went back to her apartment and a kind of grieving took place, undeclared but deeply felt. Something alive was no longer here, and she chose that and I went along with it.

The next day I suggested, "Why don't we go out and buy that stereo you wanted?"

We did just that and filled the emptiness we felt with *things*. We would always know what we did and would have to live with that choice and its consequences. I don't know how I knew, but I saw that this life was a girl and I could see her at age ten, twenty, thirty, forty. And, I longed for her, the daughter I would never have, the child I would never see. There is a sadness in me that persists through all the years that I rarely dwell on. My one chance and Sarah and I blew it. Sarah never had children and neither did I. What could have been never was.

What happens to a dream deferred?

A few weeks later, I was at Erica's apartment and Jeannie was there. Jeannie was larger than life. Wide-eyed and always smiling, beautiful and charismatic, her presence filled the room. She had the gift of explaining things in an insightful and poetic way. I mentioned the abortion to her and how guilty I felt.

Jeannie spoke, "Bob, do you really think you have control over life and death? The essence of that person, *its soul*, still exists, always will. You cannot harm it. All you did was delay its incarnation. That's all. Be at peace."

Hearing that *did* bring peace to me. I forgave myself for what I thought I'd done and thanked God for this message. A few months later, one of my favorite students confided in me that she just had an abortion, twins. She was in tears and suffering deeply. I repeated the words that gave me peace and they gave her peace, too. She looked serene for a moment and I hugged her and told her I loved her. I gave her a written pass and she went back to class. We were on this journey together. Throughout my life, I discovered that the Universe sends us who we need. Sometimes, *we* are sent to someone who needs us.

About seven months after the abortion, Sarah wanted out of the relationship. She was ready to move on. I didn't want to break up, but the die was cast. I remembered I gave it one last try, in bed. The sex was spectacular, however the next morning on that late June 1977 Sunday, she said she would not be deterred. She wanted out. It was over.

I moped around that summer in the city. One August night, my friend, Paul, and I were walking on Seventh Avenue near Bleecker. I saw Sarah walking across the street with a good-looking guy. I was livid. Paul and I went to a local pub and drank some beers.

I started my monologue; Paul listened loyally.

"Sarah and her latest boyfriend. Bitch! I hate her. It didn't take her long to get over me. A period of mourning would have satisfied me. Fuck her. In fucking two years, I knew she never got 'me.'" I wondered why she had to live around the corner from me at the Vermeer on West 14th Street.

"*Bitch*," I reiterated.

"It'll take some time, but you'll get over this, Bob," Paul reassured me.

Being with Paul, my seminarian buddy, was cathartic for me. We always had each other's back and could tell each other the truth about ourselves. I felt like shit and didn't want to go through another painful breakup. I needed to do something radical. This time it was the *est* training. *Est* was a trendy, explosive group experience with three hundred people, which promised to transform your life. Two three-day weekends and meetings in between were required. Celebrities and everyday people were joining in San Francisco, its headquarters. It was now in New York City. Trainers challenged individuals to be themselves, rather than play a role imposed on them by the past. In August, I signed up for the last two weekends in September 1977.

Later that month, I went out to dinner at the renowned Italian restaurant Gargiulo's in Coney Island with some friends. The four of us, two guys and two girls, drank four bottles of wine! We must have been very drunk, because by the time we got back to one of the women's apartment, we wound up taking off our clothes and jumping into bed. I was astounded; *everyone wanted me*. I was used to seeing myself as a sexual cripple, so this was amazing to my insecure self. Of the three of them, however, I was only interested in the guy and he was interested in me. He and I started making out and the women protested. The sizzle was extinguished, the fire put out. One of the women was married to him and she wasn't going for it. I kinda knew it would wind up this way.

September rolled around and I found that the *est* training was a composite of all the psychology and spiritual wisdom I'd heard up until then and the packaging was such that it brought about powerful results. In the middle of the second weekend, I promised myself I would be in a relationship in October. I saw it clearly. I was going to make it happen. I would be in a relationship in a very short time.

*

Jan

I met Jan at a party. No, I met her *after* a party. It was a Friday night in October 1977. A friend on the Upper West Side told me that he was having several people over and there would be lots of women. I arrived at nine p.m. After an hour or so, it was clear that this gathering of New Yorkers was a bust. People kept to themselves and didn't seem available and there wasn't a plethora of women. It was time to make a quiet exit. I went to get my coat in the bedroom when I bumped into Jan looking through a mound of coats stacked high on the bed. Jan was a handsome woman of diminutive stature with well-coiffed, reddish-brown hair. Stylishly dressed and in high heels, her ample breasts made me take notice. She was pulling out one coat after another and seemed exasperated.

"Need any help?" I ventured.

"Do the Russians like vodka?" she answered. I smiled.

"What does your coat look like?"

"It's a black leather jacket. A *female* garment."

I laughed.

"I'll help you."

Rummaging through the coats, I came across mine first. After a few moments, an arm of a black leather jacket could be seen hanging down the side of the bed.

I said, "Could this be it?"

"Yes! What a man!" she uttered *à la* Mae West. The night wasn't a total loss, or so it seemed now.

"Wasn't a great party, was it?" I asked.

"If you like attending a funeral service, it was grand."

I chuckled, "You know, I'd like to get to know you. Why don't you give me your phone number?"

She smiled broadly with eyes twinkling and said, "Sure."

Jan retrieved a scrap of paper from her purse, scribbled her name and number down, and handed it to me.

"I'll call you next week."

We walked to the elevator, went down to the lobby, and smiled at each other as we went in opposite directions.

"See ya," I said.

"Yes, looking forward to it!"

I called her up on Wednesday evening and the following Saturday night we went to a seafood restaurant in her neighborhood on Second Avenue, Pier 9. After we sat down, she ordered a glass of Chablis and I asked for Vodka Gibson, up, no vermouth. We were at a table for two and we leaned forward as we spoke. The lighting was subdued and the candles on each table flickered. We started the dance, sniffing around like two dogs getting to know each other.

"What kind of work do you do?" I asked. Small talk.

"I'm department chair of special education at Lincoln High School in the Brighton Beach section of Brooklyn. And you?" Oh, good, she works in the schools.

"I'm a counselor at Fort Hamilton High and I teach a psych course for juniors and seniors. I used to teach Latin and that paid the rent for twelve years. Then I studied to be a guidance counselor and became licensed."

I told her how much I loved teenagers, how they made me laugh all the time.

"Sounds like fun," she said.

"It is. Do you like being the boss?" I had never been a boss and had no inclination to be one. I wanted to be on the front lines.

"As Mel Brooks says, 'It's good to be the king!' in my case, the *queen*."

I laughed.

"Do you have any family?" I was hoping so.

"Well, I'm one of four, two sisters and two brothers. I'm the third child. My dad is still alive; he's a lawyer and has a Ph.D. in Economics. My mother died several years ago. Cancer."

"I'm sorry about your mother," I said. Jan looked ashen. I filled her in on my family.

"I'm the youngest of four brothers. Both my parents are living in Brooklyn. My dad has his own business on Broome Street and my mom stays at home."

I liked that she was one of four. She spoke about them and her father with great affection. I was very connected to my family; my brothers and their families lived within a ten-block radius from my parents. We always visited each other; even me from the city. Sarah was an only child and she begrudged my family. Jan was a welcomed relief.

I went in a new direction. I sat back and said, "I just came out of a two-year relationship." I explained briefly that it wasn't a pleasant parting. What I didn't tell her was how hurt and perplexed I was and that we had had an abortion and I was wrecked from the experience.

"I'm just coming out of a divorce. The papers have been filed and it'll be official in a year."

Wow, she's coming out of a break-up, too.

"So, I see we're in similar places," I said.

"Indeed."

We paused for a moment and looked at each other. Her face was kind and she had an air of acceptance in her gaze. She also had a fleeting expression of pathos; she was no stranger to pain. I liked this woman; I trusted her. Felt comfortable with her. I thought I could tell her things. Private things.

The salads came out and then red snapper and the flounder filet. We had our coffee and shared a piece of Mississippi mud cake. Afterwards, Jan invited me up to her place on Third Avenue off East 18th Street. I said, "Great." We went up to her apartment furnished with lots of custom-made cherry wood cabinetry and furniture right out of Bloomingdale's. She poured me an aperitif and brought out some Godiva truffles. We sat on the sofa. Warm and sweet and cozy. We wound up in bed and added sex to the delights of the evening. I stayed the night.

I met Jan's sister and husband in Larchmont, her older brother and his family in Greenwich, and a younger brother who seemed to be the black sheep of the family; he was an auto mechanic. Very unusual for a Jewish family. Jan met my brothers and their wives; we often went out together and had a raucous time. Italians were like that. We dated, double-dated, went to the theatre and movies, and often went out dancing. One night, we doubled with my cousin, Rob, and his girl, Angela. The women wanted to celebrate our April birthdays but it was expensive; dinner at an upscale restaurant and then dancing at *Les Mouches,* the hottest disco in town. Jan devised a plan.

In Madeline Kahn [*Blazing Saddles, Young Frankenstein*] intonations, Jan said, "We *cahn't* afford this evening because it is beyond our means. Ahfter all, Angela is a nurse and I'm a civil servant, a public *em-ploy-ee*. However, we can have a fabulous time only if we split costs."

Rob and I said we'd be game.

Now I know she divided the cost into eighths, but she preferred to use halves in this way, "Angela will pay one and a *hahf,* and I will pay one and a *hahf,* and you guys will pay a *hahf* and a *hahf*."

I said, "Let me get this straight. You women will pay one and a *hahf,* and one and a *hahf,* and Rob and I will pay a *hahf* and a *hahf*. Is that right?"

The evening arrived, and after a drink or two, we repeated the financial arrangements. The more we said it, the more hysterical we became. We ate our fill and we danced the night away. It was a fabulous time.

It became clear to me that Jan was the best woman I had ever dated. Everything worked. We laughed a lot, had hot sex anytime of the day [after all, she had those wonderful breasts], we understood the importance of family, we could talk seriously and clear up disagreements readily. We listened to each other. And because we really liked each other, people enjoyed being around us.

Chapter Eleven

Dipping My Toe in the Water,
Then a Whole Foot

One night, we were sitting in her apartment, sipping some wine after dinner and a movie.

"Jan, I want to be open about something. It's hard for me to say this, but I'd like to say it."

I was feeling on edge, nervous.

"Sure, Bob, what is it?" she asked hesitatingly.

"Well, it's something I've always thought about, but never acted on."

Just say it.

"Yes...?"

I was in it this far, so I plunged in, "I'm bisexual and think I want to experiment with my gay side."

She became pensive and said, slowly, "Okay...I don't know what to say... I guess it's better you told me." She had a faraway look. I saw it but didn't know if I could respond to it. I was relieved. I'd said it out loud. I declared my intention.

There was tension in the room. I changed the subject and we started talking about something else. We watched some T.V. and then went to bed. We had sex, talked a bit about what we might do the next day. Then finally, we retreated to sleep. The cat was out of the bag. The elephant was now in the room.

I'm not exactly sure what Jan thought about my revelation, but I knew she didn't want me to do it. I even made myself believe she thought I wouldn't do it. Maybe I presented it as a possibility, but not as a strong one, which belied my longing. After all, I was 34 and I still hadn't done it.

At this time, I was taking a ten-week seminar at *est* entitled, *About Sex*. I stood up one day and made this confession in front of the group of several hundred participants.

"I am in a relationship with a wonderful woman. We get along very well and we have good sex. She is the best woman I have ever been with. But, I'm bisexual. I have had gay feelings all my life and never did anything about them. I want to experiment but am paralyzed."

The guy sitting next to me spoke to me afterwards. He was a male model and was up for a Winston cigarette ad campaign. He told me he was exactly in the same place. Two guys unable to make a move. Not even with each other.

In the beginning of my second year with Jan, I decided to take some action.

Whenever I wanted to make a move into some new territory, I joined a group. If I wanted to be super-religious, I joined the seminary and studied to be a priest. If I wanted to get in touch with my anger, I joined the gestalt therapy center, Group Labs, on West 91st Street, where the rooms were insulated for sound and they provided Styrofoam bats called *batakas* and mats to pound on while I screamed, "I'm angry, I'm angry." Sadie and Frank got the shit beat out of them on those mats with my *bataka* because parents were obviously the cause of everything wrong in one's life. Sadie would say in dismay about shrinks, "They always blame the mothers." If I wanted to lose weight, I joined Weight Watchers, where a woman stood up and asked if eating half a carrot cake could be considered a vegetable. If I wanted to sing my heart out at Carnegie Hall, I joined the Saint Cecilia Chorus; I was a pretty good high tenor. So, I thought that if I wanted to explore my gay side, I should join a group so I joined *Both Sides Now*.

Both Sides Now met at a church on West 14th Street and Ninth Avenue. We sat in a circle in the church basement. There were two group leaders, a man and a woman. The woman spoke first.

"I'd like to welcome you to *Both Sides Now*," the female leader said. "We are a bisexual group that meets monthly."

Then the man spoke, "Our concept is that to be truly bisexual you must go out with a man and a woman at the same time."

I thought to myself, *What the fuck?*

A woman asked, "What if you want to just go out with a man and then a woman?"

The male leader said, "Go find another group."

There was a man in the group who looked like he'd been released from Bellevue Psych Ward a few hours before. He asked, "When are we going to talk about sex? I wanna talk about sex."

I thought to myself, *What the fuck?*

"We're not going to talk about sex; we're here to talk about relationships," the male leader answered.

"But I wanna talk about sex," he repeated. We all looked aghast, pretending we didn't hear what we just heard. He was ignored no matter how many times he intruded with the same inquiry.

Finally, the group ended. I couldn't find the exit fast enough.

Then I attended a group called *The Bisexual Forum* on the upper Eastside. A psychiatrist, Fred Klein, who wrote a book called *The Bisexual Option* organized it. It was an easygoing group where men and women talked about falling in love with someone whose gender was secondary to the person. Sometimes, you fell in love with a man, another time a woman. I liked this concept since I now had my feet in both worlds. I attended several meetings and was pleased with their *laissez-faire* attitude. Nothing to believe in, just love the one you're with.

That's what Stephen Stills meant!

I joined the gay Catholic group, *Dignity N.Y.C.* We'd meet in an Upper Westside brownstone where gay Jesuits, the liberal intelligentsia of the Catholic Church, would say mass. One priest also had a lover, a real cutie I thought; tall, slender, the face of an angel. Afterwards, there would be a social. It amazed me that these men were both gay and Catholic; revolutionaries within the Church trying to bring about change. So, each Saturday night, I went to gay mass in the hope of blending my Catholicism with my homosexuality. And yes, I also wanted to get laid.

So, what was it like to actively seek out what I had been vigorously suppressing all these years? I thought of the first time I dived into a pool from the high board that was ten feet up in the air. I thought of the first time I put on skis while four-year-olds glided around and behind me with unqualified ease. I thought of a first day on a new job doing something I never did before. My options were many: procrastination, paralysis, homicide, and suicide to name a few. But I had to be bigger than my fear or at least fake it, pretending I wasn't in absolute terror. I was removing the cork that secured a bottle of champagne not knowing how loud the *pop* or how much froth there would be.

I had never been comfortable meeting a new romantic possibility in social situations like bars and discos. These gatherings were too noisy for me. I'd always be shouting out something about something banal just to make contact. I didn't like it in the straight world, so why would I like it in the gay?

But this was different. It was like a party where I could have some wine, loosen up a little, and maybe even have an intelligent conversation about the last musical I saw. Besides, I had just received gay communion from a gay priest and wasn't gay Jesus on my side? So, I grabbed a plastic glass of Chablis and began to scope out the room as I moved about. There was this cute guy who was an iconic clone that all gay men tried to emulate in the late 1970s; a mustache, a short haircut, tight jeans, white sneakers, a close-fitting Lacoste polo shirt, and did I mention tight jeans? He scared me; I thought he was out of my league. I moved about the room, near him and said, "Hi," to which he responded, "Hi." He then moved on, obviously not interested. I was crushed but didn't show it; at least I hope I didn't.

Then I met this guy James. He started a conversation with me, thank God. He had a brown Afro, was fair skinned and Irish, fairly good looking with intense eyes and a huge smile as he chatted me up. After a while, we decided to go to his place in Washington Heights. His apartment had a lot of clutter, neat, but too much crammed into too little a space. It was November and so he was baking cookies and tarts and rugelach and miniature brownies and blondies by the dozens placed carefully in one-gallon bell jars. And he was just starting. By Christmas, he would have a huge inventory of goodies that he would give out as presents. I sampled a few with the tea he made for me; he was indeed a good baker.

I was nervous; this was my first time where sex with a man was probable. My internal Catholic guy was screaming out at me, "What are you doing? What are you about to do?" I told that voice to shut the hell up. I just wanted a blowjob. Was that so awful? All right, it was going to be from a man…but would galaxies collide if I came in his mouth? Then I heard the priests from my past speaking out and causing a commotion in my head.

Father Egan, when I was twelve, "Taking pleasure from impure thoughts is a mortal sin. Even putting yourself in a situation that might promote sexual arousal, is a mortal sin. You are damning your soul to eternal hellfire if you do such things."

Father Haggerty, when I was thirteen, "If you get an erection and rub your member up and down and ejaculate and waste your semen, it's a mortal sin! This is called masturbation. It is also called Onanism. Onan, in the Old Testament, was struck down by God because he wasted his semen."

Father Villani, when I was twenty-two, "Having sex outside of marriage is illicit and not permitted. This is called fornication and fornicators are committing mortal sins that will ensure everlasting damnation. Adulterers will be dealt with in the same way."

The problem was *I grew up believing this*. So here I was, at age thirty-five at this point, seated on James's sofa and contemplating an act that the Leviticus declared *an abomination*, worse than any of those sins in the straight world. What price would this sacrilege exact from my immortal soul? I told my Catholic superego to shut the fuck up and chomped on a chocolate chip cookie and sipped my tea, smiling at James all the while as we spoke and laughed. He *was* a congenial host.

However, now teatime was over. We stopped talking and there was that silent moment when you know the tide has turned. I looked at him, he looked at me and we kissed. Passionately. I unbuttoned his shirt and he unbuttoned mine and we began the touching, the *fabulous* touching and let sensuality have its way. If this was sin, let sin prevail! Soon, we were on the bed and we unbuckled our jeans and there we were about to do other things with our lips; yes, oral sex. And we did just that. To completion. After the moaning and *Omigods* subsided, and after our eyes rolled back in our heads, we just lay there in each other's arms. I liked it and knew I would revisit this tasty delight again and again. It was like the lasagna Bolognese with a *béchamel* sauce that you ordered at your favorite Italian restaurant every time you went there.

As the night progressed, we did the nasty. *My, my, my.* Where had I been all these years? Reciprocal anal sex was a blast and I thought how versatile gay sex is. And how it just hits the spot, bull's eye. I had always liked sex any way I could get it either with myself or with a woman. Sex was play and from time to time was much more especially if I were in love, like with Ana. I remembered giving her oral sex one night on the red shag rug and coming at the same time just in the act of cunnilingus. I was in love with her and this transformed sex into an intense expression of love. This night, with James, was *not* that. It was sex as play. Not that there's anything wrong with play. But play was not what I wanted ultimately; I wanted serious.

James and I lasted a couple of months as I juggled him and Jan. But soon, I grew tired of him. How shall I put it? He was a little too gay for me. Maybe too many cookies, maybe too many tchotchkes, maybe it was that his brown Afro was really a hairpiece, which he never took off in front of me. The spark was gone and though I liked him as a possible friend, it was time to move on.

I continued going to Dignity functions, but to be considered more legitimate, they got permission to hold mass at St. Francis Xavier church on West 16^{thth} Street in Manhattan. It was a frosty atmosphere with shadowy silences surrounding the altar with severe granite columns. There was something romantic about mass at a table where dinner was served in someone's brownstone that this austere place lacked. Soon, a contingent of the leather crowd started attending and some of the Dignity leadership was appalled. I thought, *Live and let live*, and if people liked rough sex and whips and wanted to receive communion, more power to them! The leadership sought to get them out. Now *I* was appalled. The oppressed were now the oppressors.

The appeal of being Catholic and gay soon lost its charm for me. These Catholics seemed as small-minded as the Church I left. I didn't want to fit my gayness into a Catholicism that was rigid and unyielding. I soon became disenchanted with Dignity and stopped going to mass. I left one oppressive system; why supplant it with another?

Being "bisexual" was more acceptable to me. It meant I was still part heterosexual. I was, in my mind, still a part of *most* of the world. Could I live in both worlds? Dr. Rubio had said that Sean, the fellow seminarian I was in love with, was only a "friend." Jack told me that my gayness was part of the furniture and I should just ignore it. But then Frayda said that my gay feelings were an integral part of who I was, that I'd always be denying myself and never be who I truly was if I ignored these feelings. At that time, I was living with Ana and I wanted to marry her and have kids. I simply tucked that notion in the back of my mind, not knowing what to do with it. So, I did nothing.

*

It was now the Spring of 1979. I was open with Jan about it all and one day, we were walking down East 15th Street.

Jan said, "I think we should break up."

She looked pale.

I said, "No."

We stayed together; she didn't leave. We weren't ready for a breakup. No, *I* wasn't ready for a break-up. I needed her to stay around, even though things were getting stale and I was heading somewhere else. I didn't care. I didn't *allow* myself to care.

I was being pulled in two directions. I came from a strong Italian family life and wanted to create a family. Wife, kids, the house with the white picket fence. *La Famiglia*! However, there was this other thing… an itch that yearned to be scratched, the piece of furniture that was ignored and not sat upon. And it tortured me. Plagued me. I had been fighting to be straight all these years, but was I gay? I loved the women in my life, loved being in love, but there was this other thing in me. The feelings I had submerged for so long I was finally allowing to surface. I wanted it out. I wanted, even hoped that Jan could be an ally.

As I explored my sexuality, I was hurting her. Jan came from a failed marriage, and now, she had me. I knew I was taking advantage of her kindness. I was straying from the caring person I thought I was as I was exploring my gay sexuality. I needed a safe haven, a friendly harbor to go back to as I was testing these new waters. I ignored her feelings and I lied to myself. I thought I could have it both ways. The voices in my head were competing with each other, vying to be the loudest. A part of me was gradually, finally emerging. A war was going on in me was projected outwards. In a war, you can't escape casualties. Someone gets hurt. In this war, Jan got hurt. I tried to believe that wasn't happening. And if I saw it happening, I ignored it.

*

I discovered an advertisement in Dignity's newsletter. "Fire Island Pines-Dignity renting house for the month of August." It was divided into five one-week shares. Joe was running the house and I told him I'd like to go for the full month. And that is what I did. Jan and I didn't vacation together. The year before I'd gone to Israel by myself. She went to California. So I told her my plan. She wasn't happy about it, but she simply said okay and devised her own August plans. On August 1st, I boarded the ferry to Fire Island Pines and entered a paradise I didn't know existed.

Fire Island Pines is one of the two gay communities on the island. It is adjacent to Cherry Grove. The Pines was very Upper East Side, snooty and well appointed. The Grove was more West Village, relaxed and maybe even a little run-down. Between the two was the infamous Meat Rack, a track of forest where you could have sex anytime of the day or night. Just take a walk. Scared the shit out of me. Just to meet somebody, not talk and just have sex. How could I do that? It was like a Catholic fasting during Lent and all of a sudden, they open a candy store and say, "Have anything you want!" I didn't know how to be in an arena where there were no clear guidelines. Here freedom was license to do whatever you wanted.

Each night, there was Tea Dance at the Blue Whale, an outdoor bar. It was off a pier where the rich and famous docked their yachts. Liz Taylor was often there partying with other celebrities like Kevin Kline or the other Klein, who had a home there. One time, I found myself standing next to Cher as I sipped my vodka tonic and another time, I wound up dancing next to Divine. Peter Berlin, the famous porn star, was often seen about. And oh yes, did I mention that there were beautiful men? It was like a Hollywood set. All these men, handsome, fit, sun-tanned, and they were *all* gay! Unbelievable. I was always in love with some guy who was in my class, or down the block and he was usually straight. No possibility. These gorgeous men were gay! Endless possibilities. Could I handle this?

Catholic gay men started arriving at the Dignity house. It was remarkable. I met men from all over the country who were going through a very similar struggle; coming out as Roman Catholics and accepting who and what they were. Week after week, a different group of men appeared. We had lots of heart-to-hearts; many of us were ex-seminarians. Some were ex-priests.

Mark was my age, maybe a little older. He had a beard that heightened his handsome looks, a winsome smile, and a soft-spoken manner. We were walking along the beach one evening heading toward Cherry Grove.

"I was studying to be a priest for almost four years," I said.

"I was a Maryknoller for almost seven years," Mark ventured, referring to the Catholic mission organization.

"Reconciling the Catholic thing and being gay is quite a trip."

"You're right. They got us as kids and mind-fucked us early on. It's hard to uproot a whole system with one that seems to be the complete opposite."

We commiserated about our Catholic upbringings; being indoctrinated that sex was bad and that only married sex was good. Forget about gay sex. That wasn't even mentioned.

"How do we get beyond all that?" I mused.

"By being here with other Catholic men who are trying to find their own truth. And unlearning all we've learned about love and sex. We're like pioneers, exploring a whole new landscape."

"And laying down a whole new life in uncharted territories."

"We'll just have to let our truth prevail and include God in our journey," I said.

My first sexual experience on the Island was with a cute boy-toy who took off his clothes readily and lay next to me in my bed. We touched each other's bodies and kissed deeply. Only he only wanted to lay back and be serviced. Not very satisfying.

I had contracted herpes years before when I was going out with a woman from Flatbush. If I was anxious, I sometimes had an outbreak. As the first week melted into the second, I had an outbreak.

One afternoon during my outbreak, a few South Americans visited someone in our house. There was this one Albaro. Everyone wanted him and guess what? He wanted me! I didn't know I could attract someone like him. He pushed me into one of the bedrooms and shoved me on the bed and started pulling off my clothes. I stopped him.

"I'm sorry, Albaro. I'm having an outbreak of herpes."

Well, that's a conversation-stopper, not to mention what it did to imminent sex. Before A.I.D.S., herpes was the scourge of the entire sexual revolution. It wasn't like today when you take Valtrex daily and never have an outbreak. Albaro appeared and disappeared. And I just sighed.

But I met other guys. There was Paul and Johnny and Rick and Michael. My herpes disappeared, thank God, and I was ready to play again. One night, I was out dancing by myself. In those days, you could simply get on the floor and dance with any friendly stranger. I had my football jersey on and tight jeans and was in cowboy boots.

All of a sudden, this really handsome guy started to dance with me. He pulled me closer to him and I liked it. Then a second man began to dance with us; he wasn't as good looking as the first. I became confused but started to realize the first guy was setting me up for a threesome. I froze. I never had a threesome! The good-looking guy noticed my fear and started to mimic what I might be thinking out loud.

"Oh my. Who is this second guy? Will I be able to handle a threesome? I don't think so," he said to me with a smirk.

His tone was unkind and demeaning, even taunting. I suddenly didn't like this guy; *God*, nasty people were everywhere. I wanted to get away; I left the dance floor. I found Paul from the other night and went home with him again. In the morning, I woke up first and noticed there was a mirror on the headboard. I looked at the two of us. I liked the way we looked. I could see myself being in love with a man, really. Paul wasn't that man, but I felt it was possible to find love in this world.

And yet men are dogs. All we want is the next lay. Our dicks are our guides. Ask any man. If he says otherwise, he's lying. It is known that straight guys would say they love a woman just to get laid. In the gay world, sex is an easy commodity. Sex is separate from love. Sex is a game and gay men play it well. Above all, gay men are *men* first! Men want to get laid and re-laid and then get laid and re-laid again. Could love be found in a world where sex is so readily available just for the asking? I've always been a romantic and always believed that love could be found anywhere under any circumstances. I believe in synchronicity and that there are no accidents. We meet the people we're supposed to meet. I was considering leaving a world I knew. I loved women and women loved me. And now I was going into this new arena. I didn't know how I would do. There was no guarantee that I would find a man to love who loved me. I was monogamous by nature and I was going into a world where sleeping with hundreds, no thousands was the way. I was afraid and ambivalent. Should I stay or move on? I was on the precipice and didn't know what to do.

*

The summer soon ended and it was now the night before Labor Day. I came home and called Jan. We arranged to see each other at her apartment. I looked forward to seeing her. We had a glass of wine and told each other about our summers. She told me she went to the Berkshires and stayed with friends and then went to East Hampton to a house she had a half-share in. I told her I went to Fire Island and met a lot of people and saw Cher and Divine and Kevin Kline and Calvin.

"It was great fun," I said. We spoke, but really didn't say too much.

I knew what I had done should not be talked about. Certainly not the excitement of self-revelation and finally, finally coming home to whom I really was. I was elated. And at the same time, I sensed an ending was soon to be; the end of a dream. It didn't include a wife and kids and all that. It saddened me. Did I want to leave that dream behind? And what about Jan? I used our relationship as a stepping-stone to a new possibility. Could I ever forgive myself? Could she ever forgive me?

It was late, so we decided to go to bed. We started kissing and I caressed her breasts and was fully turned on. But something strange started to happen. I was a little high, intoxicated from the wine and my summer. It was dark and I found myself searching for an erection. It horrified me. I simply forged ahead and had this fuck that was the hardest fuck we had ever had. We both came and Fran, sure of her standing after such a fuck, asked with a broad smile, "Well, Bob, how do you like being gay?"

I candidly answered, "I like being gay."

It just came out.

She turned white. I died a little inside. I had hurt her. Now it was clear.

"Bob, you have to go."

My eyes started to water.

"But, Jan…"

She said it again, "Bob… you…have…to…go."

Now she was tearing.

It was over. Jan did what I was afraid to do. It was the final step and I couldn't be the one to leave the relationship. She had to push me out.

And so, I went to the door and she closed it behind me. I walked to the elevator for the last time, went to the street level to my car, and drove off into my new unknown life. I was happy and I was sad. Both at the same time. After years of inner turmoil, I dared to enter the next chapter of my life; *being gay*. I didn't know how I would do it, but I *knew* I would do it.

Chapter Twelve

A Weekend in the Country

Wisdom tells me I am nothing;
Love tells me I am everything.
Between the two, my life flows.
– Nisargadatta Maharaj

It was autumn; I was thirty-six when I drove up to Woodstock for an experiential weekend retreat on sexuality. The Taconic Parkway revealed a full array of autumnal colors: dazzling yellows, deep reds, and burnished browns. The trees swayed as the leaves danced as if rejoicing, "Look at me! I'm ecstatic and having so much fun. Join me." I was certainly up for ecstasy and always down for fun. This weekend could provide both.

I drove up the path to Fred's home where the workshop was taking place. Fred Klein was a psychiatrist, the founder of The Bisexual Forum on New York's Upper East Side. I had been going to groups there for the past six months. I also read his book *The Bisexual Option*, which had recently been published.

Fred waved to me as I got out of the car; I waved back. Several people had already arrived and were relaxing on the outdoor deck with a glass of wine. Fred was a hulk of a man, tall and bald, with eyes that sparkled. He was happy to see me and I felt welcomed by his encompassing bear hug. He introduced me to the others.

First, I shook hands with Ahmed, who was second in command at the forum. He was dark complexioned and his brown eyes that peered out from under narrow but sharply defined eyebrows looked at you and noticed everything about you. His smile revealed a full set of white teeth and he seemed to smirk, which put me a little on edge. He oozed sexuality and his girlfriend, Alice, was indeed lucky. She had lovely cascading auburn hair, an appealing smile and a pretty face; her eyes generated warmth. She held out her hand and said, "Nice to meet you."

Then there was MaryAnn whom I had met previously at meetings. She was a diminutive bundle of dynamite. She had the charisma of a rock star and you couldn't help but want to be a roadie for her act. She was in the S&M scene and provided her services as a dominatrix privately and as a staff member at Belle de Jour's *The Loft* in Chelsea, the first of its kind in New York City. MaryAnn had a huge, ingratiating smile and eyes that widened as she said hello. We hugged each other.

Beside her was Haikila, whom I knew from meetings as well. She and MaryAnn were close, sometime lovers, always friends. Haikila was a woman of considerable magnitude, not fat, just substantial. She was Gaia, Mother Earth. Her face was regal and compelling. Her luminous eyes could make you feel that everything was going to be all right, don't worry, love surrounds you. Her heart had its door swung wide-open and I happily walked right in. Everyone did.

Billy was a Southern boy in his early thirties who just came in from Fort Lauderdale. He originally came from Tuscaloosa and his drawl and Southern gentility won me over. He was powerfully built, fair-skinned and handsome as his blue eyes and smile welcomed me. His sandy hair flew in the wind, making his gentlemanly appearance a little unkempt, which made him more attractive. He shook my hand with vigorously and said, "Bob, nice ta meet y'all." I melted like butter in the nooks and crannies of an English muffin just out of the toaster. I managed to respond, "Same here, Billy."

Matteo, a tall Italian guy from Brooklyn, was a little bit of all right. He actually lived with his girlfriend, Laura, around the corner from my brother, Ron, on East 27th Street. He was naturally dark-skinned, had curly black hair, and brown eyes that pierced right through me; he also had a killer smile.

I thought, *Yummy,* as I shook his hand. I knew him from meetings, but this Friday, afternoon, in Woodstock, on this deck, he looked particularly appealing. His gregariousness was contagious and he unassumingly exuded sexuality.

Another car arrived. A tall guy unfolded himself out of the driver's seat and bounded up the stairs and made his presence known. His name was Myron, a bit awkward, a little too loud, and much too intense. When shaking hands, he stood just a little too close, enough to make me uncomfortable. His display of neediness annoyed me. I took an instant dislike to him.

Late afternoon became evening and as the sun was setting, Fred ushered us to our rooms. As it turned out, the gods put Billy and me in the same bedroom. We unpacked and freshened up and since it was now suppertime, we went into the huge country kitchen for a pleasant repast. Alice and Ahmed were our chefs for the weekend. Fred told us we would have our first workshop session after dinner.

During our meal, we were asked to answer the following question, "What brought you here this weekend?"

As we passed the large multi-lettuce salad, the freshly baked breads, the spinach *sautéed* in olive oil and garlic, the mashed potatoes, and the grilled lime salted salmon filets, one by one, we responded.

MaryAnn said her focus was on relationship while Matteo said he was living with his girlfriend who wanted to get married while he was struggling with his attraction to men. Matteo passed the mashed potatoes to Haikila who wanted to explore how love and sexuality intertwine.

Ahmed told us his problem was only going so far with intimacy, whether with Alice or a male lover.

"I want to know how to transcend my fear," he said taking a piece of salmon from the serving plate. "Alice said she was in conflict."

She wanted to be monogamous with Ahmed and nest, maybe even have a child. She was tired of playing around with both sexes and wanted to just be with Ahmed.

As I dipped my bread into peppered olive oil, I told the group that I was new to the gay scene, that I spent the summer in Fire Island Pines and broke up with my girlfriend, Jan, a few months back.

"I'm in my second adolescence and seeking love in hopefully all the right places. I need a friendly and safe space to talk about it. The Bisexual Forum always provided that for me."

I passed the spinach over to Billy who told us he was originally from Tuscaloosa and was brought up in an evangelical Southern Baptist home where he was taught that sex leads you on the path to hell and that homosexuality is the abomination that ignites the flames.

"I've got a girlfriend, Addison, but I like men, too. I don't know what to do. I'm hoping this weekend will push me along."

Myron spoke next.

"I'm gay, was always gay, and will always be gay. I have no interest in women. I'm looking for a lover. Maybe I'll find one this weekend. Ha-ha," he snickered.

I cringed. He made my skin crawl.

Fred was the last to speak. He spoke about sexuality as flexible and supple, according to one's desires. He explained the Kinsey Scale that goes from 0 to 6. "Some people are pure heterosexuals or pure homosexuals, a zero or a six on the scale. But most of us reside between two and five, and as a result our sexuality is more flexible. We'll talk about our sexuality openly and freely. I will be learning along with you. We'll teach each other."

After everyone spoke, I felt both somewhat comfortable and somewhat apprehensive. I was new at this gay thing and really didn't know where the weekend would lead me. I was excited and scared, but happy to be here. These were nice people and some of them were particularly hot.

We chatted about our lives and after the last morsel was eaten and the dishes put into the dishwasher, we assembled in the living room in a circle. There was a platform in our midst, maybe eight inches off the floor. We sat down on the rug and waited for Fred to start the proceedings.

Fred cleared his throat and said, "We're going to start the weekend with a body image exercise. I'm going to ask each of us to take off our clothes totally. One by one, we'll stand on the platform and tell what we like about our body."

We looked at each other apprehensively.

I thought to myself anxiously, *I can do this. Wasn't I the first to undress when six of us friends went to the nude beach in Santa Cruz in 1972?*

Emboldened by that memory, I started taking off my clothes, shoes, and socks first. Then my shirt, my jeans, finally my underwear. It wasn't that I was an exhibitionist; I was just feeling audacious. Truth be told, I never felt comfortable in my body and this exercise was no exception. I was a man trapped in another man's body. I was supposed to get the tall one with six-pack abs, and slender waist, a dancer's body or at least that of a swimmer, but I didn't. My body had muscular arms and shoulders and my legs were powerful. I worked hard at working out but I knew it could change in a month from now. The love handles, the soft belly, the fat layered pecs. Even when I was in great shape, and this was one of those times, I still felt fat. I couldn't exchange the Scherma body real or imagined at the moment, so I had to make do with what I had. I joined the others as we sat down again in a circle. I tried to appear relaxed. It was, after all, the late 1970s and the sexual revolution was in full swing.

Fred spoke, "Who's going to be the first to get up there and tell us what you like about your body?"

Nobody.

Then, somebody. MaryAnn got up to a round of applause. She said she liked her tits and her ass. We applauded more loudly, especially when she prominently displayed her aforementioned body parts.

Haikila got up and performed a ballet of sorts around the stage. She was magnificent in her stoutness, Mother Earth summoning us to her valleys and mountainous regions. Come home to Mother! We adored her.

Billy got up and he got a huge round of applause as he showed us his muscular arms and shoulders, his slimmed torso and perfectly shaped buttocks. The man, though shy and reserved, was a 10!

Others got up, one by one and so did I.

"What parts of your body do you like, Bob?" Fred asked.

The only thing I could think was my calves.

"I love my calves," I blurted out.

I was a jogger and I loved my calves. That was it. I got mild applause and sat down. Sitting down, I thought, *Wait a minute, I forgot to mention my legs. And my arms. And my neck. And the back of my hands. What about my face? Is it impolite to talk about sexual organs?*

But the opportunity had passed; it was too late. There was no do-over.

After the presentations, we discussed how we regarded our own bodies and how others saw them. If you loved your body and looked great, this was an easy conversation for you. Certainly not for me. I always had issues with my body even when I was trim, handsome, and gorgeous. Maybe it was all that Italian food causing my weight to fluctuate. Maybe it was the Catholic disdain for the body deep in the recesses of my mind. Maybe it was that I went to school too often for another degree and stopped devoting myself to the gym like my gay confreres.

Within me, I heard these recriminations:

"You're not that good-looking!"

"You have love handles!"

"You don't have a flat stomach!"

Finally, a voice within me told me, "Sit down!"

I wasn't listening to the discussion. I'd blocked it out like a survivor does with traumas forgotten and submerged. It was only Friday night and I had a weekend to contend with. I snapped out of it. I girded my loins and pressed on.

We put on shorts and tee shirts and drank some tea. We chatted, we laughed, and soon it was getting time to go to bed. There was a nice feel to this group, inviting and sensual at the same time. Everyone went to bed, except Billy, Matteo, and me. While we were chatting, another conversation, a subterranean one, was surfacing.

Matteo smiled at Billy and me. We smiled back. Matteo said, "I'm stuck with Myron. Do you mind if I stay with you guys?"

Billy and I looked at each other and said simultaneously, "Sure! Absolutely!"

It was 11:30 p.m. when we went to our room and closed the door behind us.

This autumn we were experiencing an Indian summer and the heat was on. However, in that bedroom, on that night, with a cast of three, the temperature soared as we delighted in the pleasures each body gave to the other two. We took off each other's clothes and began kissing. We kissed one and then the other and the one not kissing touched the two gently but with purpose. We pleasured each other that night with our hands, stroking the one then the other, with our mouths devouring all we could. We were insatiable. Matteo entered Billy and I entered Matteo, it was a symphony of sensuality, each of us playing each other like an instrument. Even though Billy found it hard to maintain an erection, we touched each other *con passione* and *con amore*. We experienced a crescendo after a thematic development and then a decrescendo. We were a woodwind trio and a polyphonic threesome. All we needed was the clashing of cymbals, which I think I heard. *Oh, what a night it was.*

At breakfast the next morning, Haikila looked at the three of us who apparently were in afterglow. She said to MaryAnn, "Those boys…"

MaryAnn smiled a knowing smile with one eyebrow arched.

In subsequent sessions, we spoke about relationship, and what was the same and different about being with a man or with a woman. We gave each other massages with herbal oils. We talked, then ate, and then talked again. Soon it was bedtime. The three of us retired after saying good night to the others and Haikila, smiling at us, said, again, "Those boys…"

We closed the bedroom door and after a moment or two, somebody was knocking insistently.

Knock, knock, knock.

Matteo opened the door. It was Myron.

"Myron, what's up?" Matteo asked pointedly.

"I'd like to join you tonight," he said.

We looked at each other and knew that was never going to happen. What we wanted didn't include too-pushy, too-in-your-face Myron.

I said, "Myron, this isn't going to work out. I'm going to have to say no."

"Can't I please come in?"

Now he was begging.

"It's not a good idea. Good night, Myron," Billy said.

He didn't insist and for a moment, we felt sorry for him but we recalled that he really was creepy. Guilt put aside, we went on with our evening's events.

The three-ring circus was back in town again.

On Sunday morning, we had one last breakfast and then a last session. Fred asked, "What did we learn this weekend?"

Matteo spoke up first, saying, "I see that I really like men, especially these two men right here! I hope to continue seeing them after this weekend."

Billy then said, "Being raised in the Deep South hasn't put out the fire. I love women, but I love men. Particularly, Bob and Matteo. I hope we visit each other and continue our relationship."

I spoke next, "This has been a wonderful weekend for me. Not only the loving support of friends, but a newfound relationship with Billy and Matteo. I want to continue seeing them as well. I learned that I just want to go with the flow and see where it leads me. I'm so glad I came this weekend."

I blushed when I realized what I just said.

Others gave their observations and soon the morning session was over. It was unanimous. The weekend was a success. Except for Myron, he didn't find a lover. It was time to hit the road.

We packed up, thanked Fred for his generosity and guidance, hugged each other, and got in our cars. Before Matteo got in his car, Billy and I hugged him. We exchanged phone numbers and I told Matteo I'd call him the next week. He drove off. Since Billy didn't have a car, I offered to drive him to LaGuardia for his late afternoon flight.

We got into the car and after going over the weekend's events and talking about our jobs, our friends, and our families, we arrived at American Airlines.

"Billy, I really loved meeting you this weekend," I said as I helped him with his luggage at curbside.

He smiled back at me and said, "I feel the same way, Bob. I definitely want to see you again. And Matteo, too. I come up to the city every so often for business and so let's make it happen."

I said, "Definitely! You can stay with me. Just let me know."

I smiled at him as he said, "See you real soon, Bob. I mean it."

We hugged and he went off.

I smiled back and drove off dreamily thinking of the triple encounters of the last two nights. I liked Matteo a lot, but there was something about Billy that elicited deeper feelings. I believed I was falling for the guy.

Chapter Thirteen

The Men in My Life

Billy

I went back to work at Fort Hamilton High School that next week and caught myself smiling a lot as I walked down the halls, greeting students and staff, conferring with teens in the guidance office or teaching students in my psych class.

"Mr. Scherma, you seem so happy," a student remarked.

I smiled and simply responded, "Yep."

Matteo and I got together the following Friday night at my place. His girlfriend, Laura, gave her reluctant consent. We had a bite to eat, made love, chatted, watched a little T.V., and then went to sleep. We got up the next morning and after morning sex, I saw he was antsy.

I asked, "Matteo, what's the matter?"

He answered, "I told Laura I'll be back by noon." This meant he had to leave within the hour to get back to Brooklyn on time. I sighed.

"Okay, Matteo. Do what you have to do. I'd like to meet Laura sometime."

"Give it a little time. She's adjusting to this," he said.

We had a cup of coffee and soon Matteo was gone, heading to Brooklyn on the D train.

In the meantime, Billy and I were speaking often on the phone.

"Bob, I'm going to be up in New York in two weeks. Can the three of us get together?"

"I'll make it happen. Stay with me and we'll all meet here."

I called Matteo and since we were meeting weekly, it was an easy fix. Two weeks rolled by and Billy was at my door. Matteo hadn't arrived yet.

119

Billy came into the apartment and put his overnight bag down and began kissing me. We couldn't keep our hands off each other but we decided to slow down, have a glass of wine, and wait for Matteo.

A half hour later, Matteo arrived. After, "Hello," we took off each other's clothes and luxuriated in sensuality. We were hot for each other and it was time to put out the fire. We did. Billy continued to have erection problems but was happy to serve his friends. Exhausted, we lay back on the bed and chatted and sipped some Beaujolais. What business brings you up here? How are the kids at school? How's Laura? We had a lot to talk about and a lot to do.

Saturday morning rolled around and Matteo went into restless mode.

"I gotta get back to Brooklyn. Laura's having a hard time with this."

"Okay, Matteo. Don't want to get the girlfriend angry," Billy said.

"Yeah, *don't* get the girlfriend angry," I reiterated somewhat irritated by this usual occurrence.

Matteo left by ten a.m. and Billy and I had brunch in the Village and then shot up to midtown for a Saturday matinee. We played the entire weekend, outdoors and in.

"Billy, I love having you here."

"I love being here," Billy rejoined. There was such earnestness in his words that I couldn't help but become more infatuated with him. He really liked being with me and I with him.

During one visit, some old demons visited. The three of us were naked in bed together. Matteo and Billy were really going at it and I was lying on the side of the bed feeling excluded. Ancient pain rose up of being the guy nobody wanted to be with. It had to do with the moment, but it was pain I knew from the past. It heralded back to the days when I was eight or nine. I felt that my cousin, who had recently moved upstairs, was taking over all my friends. My reaction was to stay at home, not go out after school, and not engage with others. They didn't want me anymore. They wanted him. I was really upset and Billy noticed and asked what was the matter.

"I don't know… I feel on the outside…and it hurts…and I'm sorry for spoiling the moment. I really feel bad. Unloved. Outside…" I started to tear up.

Billy spoke, "Bob, I don't want you to feel like that. You are so loveable. Everybody knows it. You have loads of friends and family who love you. Our

120

friends at the Bisexual Forum love you. The kids you work with adore you. And Matteo and I love you. Don't feel unloved, Bob, we love you."

Matteo was quiet during all this and seemed annoyed. He just wanted to get it on. But Billy spoke to my pain. He grabbed me and kissed me and held me close. It was at that moment I totally fell for Billy. We went back to the task at hand and had sex and for Billy and me, lovemaking.

We continued our threesome through January. Matteo stayed with me almost every Friday night to Saturday. We were fuckbuddies with little emotional depth, yet we liked each other's company. We were essentially friends who had sex. Matteo would leave each Saturday at ten a.m. and go back to his girlfriend, Laura. Billy came up to New York every four weeks or so.

One Friday, Matteo came up for his usual overnight. He seemed distracted. Sex was becoming routine and the thrill was gone. Saturday morning, Matteo seemed preoccupied like he had something to say.

Joe spoke up, "Laura doesn't like me seeing you and Billy anymore. It's getting to her. She doesn't like sharing me with you guys."

"So, what do you need to do, Matteo?" I asked candidly, sympathetically.

He said, "I think in order to keep peace with Laura, I've got to stop seeing you both. I'll call up Billy."

Not really surprised, I said, "Okay, Matteo. We'll stop the sex and just be friends. I still want to meet Laura and now it'll be…easier."

"I think you're right, Bob."

After three months, the threesome became a twosome and it was fine with me. Time passed as Billy and I saw each other as often as we could. I went down to Fort Lauderdale and he came up to New York. We stayed with each other for long weekends and occasionally for a week or two in Florida. He was a lovely man and I liked being around him. He also gave great head. He continued to see his girlfriend, Addison, at home and I continued to see a couple of guys regularly. There was Joey and Rick, a short dalliance with a guy named Greg, and Mike. I loved those boys to one degree or another but was in love with Billy. I wasn't counting on this to turn into something other than what it was. I knew that this Southern boy was insurmountably guilty over his homosexuality. I just liked the guy. A lot.

One day Billy told me about the South and gay boys. In his southern drawl, he explained, "Down in Tuscaloosa, a lot of my male friends have had sex with each other over the years. We see it as just being sexual. If Southern boys don't kiss, it's not homosexual. They can do everything else, but kissing is out. *That's* considered gay."

"So what we do is really *gay* according to the code of the south."

"Yes, it is," Billy admitted. A look of shame ran across his face.

"So, how do you do it, Billy?"

"I just like being with you and that's what I concentrate on," he answered.

It was such a contrast. Here's Billy, at heart a Baptist kid from Tuscaloosa, riddled with guilt about his homosexuality and unable to break out of the restrictions installed by hell-and-fire ministers. Then there was me who struggled with the same demons only installed by the Catholic Church. I had so many crushes on men all my life and couldn't act on those feelings. Now, I could. I was a New Yorker who'd stepped into the sexual revolution, gay life all around me. I was determined to free myself of the shackles that bound me and bask in my newfound sexual freedom. Billy tried but couldn't fully cross the finish line.

It was now April 1984 and Billy gave me a call. He said he had some news.

I asked, "Billy, what is it?"

"I got engaged to Addison this past week. We're getting married in two months and I want you to come down to the wedding."

I was taken aback and was surprised at my reaction. I said, "I don't know if I can come to the wedding. I can't even afford the flight and the hotel; grad school has really depleted my finances."

But that wasn't it.

"I'll pay for it; I really want you there," Billy countered.

"No, Billy. Let me think about it."

A delaying tactic.

I asked Billy, "How did you decide to marry Addison?"

"Well, I thought it was time to make a move. And Addison was a-chompin' at the bit."

"Do you want to start a family?" I asked.

"Yes, I do. We do."

"What about the gay thing?" I inquired.

"Well, I'm just going to stop playing around with it. It's too difficult. I need to get married," Billy said.

I knew his Southern Baptist indoctrination was at variance with his gay side. His erectile dysfunction spoke to that. He could perform with women; he couldn't with men.

A few weeks later, Billy came to New York and met me at my apartment. He spoke about the wedding and the music he wanted to have played. He needed a song from *West Side Story*, I happened to have the sheet music.

"Billy, you can have it," I offered. He wanted the score to "One Hand, One Heart." Ironic.

"Bob, I really want you to come down and be there," he implored.

"Billy, I can't. I just can't. It's a feeling thing. I can't watch you get married. I want the best for you, for a happy life. I just can't be there. I want only good things for you and Addison," I said.

Billy and I languished and lingered in an embrace, almost not wanting to let go. He smiled a diffident, reticent smile and kissed me goodbye.

I said, "I love you, Billy."

"I love you, too, Bob."

I closed the apartment door and heard him enter the elevator as he faded away.

I never saw or heard from Billy again.

*

Blonde God

It was my first time in the iconic St. Mark's Bathhouse off the Bowery. I was 36 and this was my first such outing. My friend, Bob, an older, more experienced namesake and guide in the gay life took me around on a tour. Here were the orgy rooms, all in the dark with bunks like shelves. Here were the steam rooms where you could get sex going with a mere look. Here were the showers, where in a moment, you could completely abandon polite demeanor and participate in a riot of sexual happenings. Then there were the individual rooms where guys were sitting or lying down spread-eagled.

Bob said, "Come over here, Bob, I have something for you to do that needs to be done."

He brought me to a room where I discovered this bear of a guy in black leather with his backside exposed and a paddle at his side. Bob gave him a couple of whacks, hard.

Then, apparently, it was my turn, "Go ahead, Bob."

"Go ahead what?" I asked.

"He needs to be whacked. Go ahead, whack him. Hard."

I thought to myself, *Oh my,* as I picked up the paddle and *Whack! Whack!*

The guy lying down looks up at me and says, "It's not hard enough."

I go at it again…and again. Still, I got a dirty look from the guy lying down as he yelled out, "Not hard enough!"

I just couldn't get it right.

I handed over the paddle to my friend Bob and said, "Here, Bob, you do it again…uh. I gotta go."

As I left the room, I heard the guy who was being whacked moan out loud, "Oh…Oh…Oh…"

I got out of there fast and thought, *I suck at this!*

And then I thought, "Let me look around. Maybe I can find something I don't suck at…"

I went to the showers and there was this blonde god with blue eyes, a killer smile, a chiseled body. I just had to touch him, make out with him, and do other things with him. Apparently, he felt the same way about me. Others joined the love fest.

*

Rick

I met Rick at a gay relationship seminar. The group leader asked us to get up and form two circles. As an icebreaker exercise, we roamed the room in our circles and said hello to as many people as we could. I was in one circle and this man, who had a crowd-pleasing smile, was in the other. He was tall and slender, wore tight blue jeans, and a loose a blue crew neck sweater. We kept on bumping into each other as we made the circuit and smiled and laughed and chatted. I was interested. As the evening progressed, we managed to sit next to each other on the floor. When the seminar was over, we walked out together.

"Hi, my name is Bob."

"Hi, my name is Rick."

"This was a great seminar, Rick, what do you think?"

"It was…and now it's even better…"

"Why don't we exchange numbers and see each other soon?"

"I'd like that, Bob"

My loins were on fire. He not only seemed to be a sweet guy, but he was also hot. I could imagine his body next to mine and the things we could do to each other. I was definitely fired up.

A week later, we went out to dinner in his neighborhood near Columbia University. I ordered a vodka Gibson and Rick a glass of chardonnay.

"What kind of work do you do, Rick?"

"I teach piano to kids and adults and I work in piano bars from time to time."

"Where did you study music?"

"At the Manhattan School of Music, down the block from where I live. What kind of work do you do, Bob?"

"I'm a college adviser at Columbus High in the Bronx. I love the work. I love teens."

We soon placed our orders. Each of us wanted a salad; Rick, a mixed greens and me, a Caesar's. I ordered two crab cakes and Rick asked for the red snapper fillet. As the meal moved forward, we chatted about music, teenagers, and politics. We were feeling comfortable with each other.

"Tell me about your relationships, Bob"

I told him I had been straight for ten years and lived with a woman and then had two other relationships with women after that. It was when I went to Fire Island Pines that I found out where I belonged, in the gay world. I mentioned I had a boyfriend or two. Then Rick told me he was always gay and had been in two serious relationships. One lasted three years and the other four.

"I think it's good to have a past. Apparently, we each have one," I ventured.

"Yes, indeed."

"What are you looking for these days?" I asked.

"A friend. Somebody to play with."

"I'd like to be that friend, Rick."

He looked up, flashed that killer smile, and turned red. Me, I was feeling bold.

"Let's go to my place, Bob."

"I'd love to."

We called the waiter over, paid the bill, and walked a few blocks down Broadway to his apartment near West 122nd Street.

Rick opened the door, I followed. We took off our jackets and he hung them up. We sat on a sofa in the living room.

"Would you like some wine?"

"No, I'm good."

He leaned over and kissed me. He was luscious. We held each other close and continued to kiss. Passionately. Soon, our shirts were off.

Then our shoes and socks. Finally, our pants.

"Let's go into the bedroom."

"Sure."

We lied down on the bed and continued to kiss and touch each other with purpose. Soon, our underwear was off and our mouths did their assigned jobs. We came readily and just lay in each other's arms, quiet and content. We pulled back the coverings and fell asleep.

A few hours later, we were aroused by passion and our erections told us what we wanted to do next. First, he did me and then I did him. Anal intercourse was never so good. We were very compatible. Our sex reminded me of what I had with Amelia almost ten years earlier. Hit the spot every time. I knew I had struck gold again with Rick.

We saw each other for the next year and a half before I went to Yeshiva University for my doctoral studies. The sex was phenomenal. We just knew exactly what to do with each other's body. The chemistry was there. We were so lucky.

As time passed by, Rick became more in love with me than I was with him. He would gaze at me, and sigh. He felt something for me that I didn't feel for him. I loved him but wasn't in love with him. Our passion was hot and had nothing to do with how we felt about each other, at least from my perspective. But it wasn't fair to Rick. I had to call it off and I did with some regret. I wasn't ready for a commitment to Rick. That was part of it, but not all of it. I always felt that I needed a little bit of a challenge. Maybe Rick was too open, too available, too in love with me. It made me uncomfortable. *And* I knew I wasn't in love with him.

*

It was sultry this summer in late July. I went to the Blue Whale, ordered a vodka and tonic, tipped the bartender, and turned around to survey the scene. It was Tea Dance in Fire Island Pines. A few men were on the dance floor already, the music was so inviting. Others stood around the outdoor deck in animated conversations, while some remained standing at the bar, like me. There was much eye candy to behold; men tanned from a day in the sun, or guys parading their product after a few hours at the gym. Sensuality was in the air as the D.J. moved the music from mellow and soulful to a more pulsating rhythm. It was like this every evening. You got to tea dance around 6:30 p.m., had a couple of drinks, danced with anyone on the dance floor, and maybe walked to the bay to watch the sunset before dinner. Sometimes, you arranged a hook up. It was an open and carefree time. It was 1980.

This Monday evening, I surveyed the dance floor and spotted this cute guy, a younger man. He was somewhat tall and slim and bronzed, had curly dark hair, and brown eyes. A square jaw defined his handsome face and his smile made him eye-catching. He danced with a tambourine, which he struck to the rhythm. I couldn't take my eyes off him. I started to dance and eventually danced closer to him. Our eyes met and we smiled. We started to dance together and the energy between us was electric. It was a good half hour when the music stopped and we introduced ourselves. Since we were walking in the same direction home, we started to chat. It was clear we liked each other, so we set up a date to meet at midnight at the local club, The Pavilion.

We met there, got a drink, and then danced the night away. Toward the end of the evening around 3 a.m. or so, the music, which was aptly called "sleaze," began to slow down. We started slow dancing. Our tanned and wet bodies pressed against each other, feeling each other, touching each other, kissing each other. We had to go home.

We made it that night and even made time to talk. I found out that his name was Hunter, age 25, from a small town in Illinois with a mid-Western sensibility and gentility that I relished. He smiled easily and spoke with a charming slight drawl. I told him I was 37, worked as a teacher and counselor in high school. We talked and made love and made plans to see each other the next night.

The week went by and we saw each other continuously. By mid-week, we were totally enamored of each other. By week's end, he told me he was heading for New York City to go clubbing until he left New York for Illinois on Wednesday.

"Bob, why don't you join me?" Hunter asked.

I said, "Great idea. You can stay with me at my place in the Village."

"Super!"

He stayed with me three nights and we visited gay haunts like The Anvil, The Cock Ring, Badlands, Crisco Disco, and The Spike. We partied, had sex, and spent all our time together. Soon, it was Wednesday and Hunter had to go home. He got in a cab and I had to get to a job interview up in the Bronx. I didn't know how I was going to get through this interview at Columbus High School. I got myself ready as I listened to Stephen Sondheim's "Losing My Mind" over and over again on the stereo.

I was a goner. Totally obsessed. And apparently, so was he.

Then came the nightly phone calls from Illinois and our declarations of love. We had to see each other again. We decided to meet in Chicago for Columbus Day Weekend.

We hadn't seen each other since August 6th and now it was Friday, October 10th and he picked me up at the airport. It felt a little awkward, like we had to get reacquainted. We checked into the hotel, had a bite to eat at a local restaurant, and returned to our room. We made love and soon started to feel at home with each other. The next day we explored the city, had brunch, and reclined near the Lake of Peacefulness, Lake Michigan. It was sweet, and warm and hot. We went dancing that night and that heated things up between us even more.

Hunter was much more into drugs than I and asked if I wanted to drop acid. I hesitated. I had done it once before and nothing special happened, nothing freaky, so I said okay. We each took a tab, ingested it, and waited.

On this Sunday afternoon, we were in our hotel room; Hunter was lying on the bed and I was sitting in an armchair. The drug kicked in and started to do its magic. We told stories from our past; family, friends, girlfriends, and boyfriends. We laughed about things from work. After a while, the conversation took a serious turn. Hunter told me about a girlfriend who had done him wrong and the story was so compelling that both of us were weeping. I told him about Ana whom I was so in love with that I thought I'd marry her and have kids. More tears.

We spoke about us. How we wanted to be together. How we wanted to be in the same city. I told him to come live with me in New York City. He hemmed and hawed and I knew his family demands included a future with a wife he hadn't met yet and certainly not with a male lover. I asked him to take the risk. I wondered if he would or even could.

How close and intimate and comfortable we were with each other. I can't quite explain it, but I felt we went through a complete relationship from start to finish in three days. The acid speeded things up and allowed for feelings to arise that would have taken months, maybe years, to emerge, much less express. We were present to each other, exposed. And how we wanted each other!

We started to feel the longing because days and hours were dwindling down and on Monday, I would be departing. Hunter drove me to O'Hare and stayed in the waiting area until I had to board the plane. We said goodbye without touching except for a handshake and a hug. As he left with a smile, he waved back and said, "See you, Bob."

I thought this was the last time I would ever see him. Just a hunch.

I got on the plane, got back to J.F.K. at eight p.m., and was picked up by my friend, Erica, in her V.W. bug and we went to the Riviera Café on West 10th Street for a drink and something to eat. I told her how wonderful the time was with Hunter.

What I couldn't tell her at the time was how lonely I would feel as days turned into weeks and weeks into months and speaking on the phone with Hunter would at first be frequent and then less and less, and finally not at all. A relationship has to go somewhere and cannot just be suspended in mid-air. If it doesn't move forward, it recedes and fades away. Slowly.

The longing continued its tortuous path.

Then I met Lucas.

*

Lucas

It was a Friday night in 1980 when I went to a Halloween Party held in a loft space in the Village. I arrived with my friend, Zell, who was dressed in a nun's habit. I hated costume parties but managed to come as a jock of some sort. I wore a blue and red football jersey with the number 33 emblazoned across my chest, blue running shorts, gray New Balances, and my old 1959 Lafayette High School football jacket. After getting a drink and saying hello to a few people, Zell introduced me to her friend, Lucas. He was tall and handsome in his pirate's costume with a white shirt and black vest, as well as a sash and belt with buckles covering his black pants and boots. He even had an eye patch. His voice was deep, mid-western, gentle, and sexy; he was seductive in an unassuming, natural way. He was totally hairless due to a medical condition and yet extremely attractive and exotic; I couldn't keep my eyes off him. His mid-western temperate and tender manner charmed me as he told me I reminded him of Al Pacino. Good line, which I completely bought. As the evening progressed, we kept on talking and flirting and smiling and gazing at each other when the other wasn't looking.

Soon it was time to go home and he and I went over to the coat rack, where I hung my football jacket earlier only to find out that it was gone. To make matters worse, my apartment keys were in its pocket. I was in shock. Who would steal my jacket? This was a Halloween party sponsored by a New Age group, *A Course in Miracles*.

Lucas spoke up, "Why not come to my place?

"You can sleep the night and then go about getting into your apartment tomorrow."

I looked at him with a little grin and said, "Sure."

We walked about fifteen minutes to what I thought was his place on Thompson Street. Instead, it was a bath and soaps shop he owned. We entered, started to kiss, and subsequently had stand-up sex.

Afterwards, he took me around the corner to his street level apartment on Sullivan Street He got me some bedding and ushered me into a children's room. He said goodnight and went to the main bed where his wife was roused from her sleep. There were two children sleeping, one a newborn. I was introduced as "a friend."

The next morning his family was out at Washington Square Park while Lucas made me breakfast. He spoke about his wife and kids in a matter-of-fact way. One thought came up, *How sophisticated!*

Another thought, *This is fucked up.*

All I knew was I was enamored of him as I went over to kiss him. However, he pulled back. I didn't see much of a future here; too complicated. He lent me a sweater and I went to my cousin, Rob, and got a second set of apartment keys and went home. I took off the sweater and held it close. I put it to my nose; it smelled of Lucas. Enough. I continued with my day. There was another Halloween party in Brooklyn that night and another younger cute guy, sexy Greg with the beard, would be there. I made ready for that as I called a locksmith to change the locks to my apartment on West 13th Street.

Months passed and Lucas became a pleasant but distant memory, a one-night stand, well played; not the hottest sex, but hot enough. Then one evening, the following January at an *A Course in Miracles* class I was attending, Lucas appeared. We were in my friend Zell's apartment on West 100th Street off Broadway; she was running the class. He was wearing a lush, white, hand-knit, Irish wool, crewneck sweater and he just looked gorgeous. He sat right next to me and a tinge of sexual energy ran through me. We exchanged ideas about the *Course* and though we listened to others speak, we were attentive to each other's every move. I was sunk, hook, line, and sinker. So was he.

We went to my place, barely entered the apartment when we tore off each other's clothes. The temperature in the room soared; we couldn't keep our hands off each other. And so it was as the months rolled by. Hot sex is hot sex.

At first, we'd meet surreptitiously at my place. But by the middle of February, I told him this arrangement wasn't working for me. He had to tell his wife, Cindy, that he was seeing me; I told him I wasn't going to run around ducking and hiding like an adolescent.

He did tell his wife who had no choice seemingly but to allow our affair to go on or lose him. We saw each other openly as the sex got hotter and hotter. It was the sticky adhesive that glued us together.

One day in March, Lucas came to my apartment with his baby for a visit and broke down in tears. He told me he was leaving his wife and wanted to be with me. I welcomed it. Then on another day in April, he told me that he didn't want to break up his family and that he couldn't leave his wife.

This back and forth became a repetitive theme as the months passed. Luckily summer was near, and I'd be going to Fire Island Pines to *not* be in the thick of this affair. Other guys would distract me, and for a while, they did.

It was now Labor Day weekend and we spent the time together at my place in the city. His wife, Mandy, was on a spiritual retreat returning Monday night. Lucas went home to be with her upon her arrival.

On Tuesday morning, I got a phone call. Lucas said there was something he wanted to tell me.

I asked, "What is it?"

He said, "Oh, nothing special. I just want to see you tonight, I'll tell you then."

It was the day before I returned to Columbus High School as college adviser and a week before I started my doctoral studies at Yeshiva University. I played a lot of Peter Allen music that had a melancholic feel to it as I prepared for my return to work. The end of summer always made me blue. Something unsaid in Lucas's words made me apprehensive.

Lucas came over that night. I really looked my best; tan and buff in white tank top and white Adidas shorts. He entered beaming.

"Mandy came back from her retreat. She was so elated and beautiful that I made a decision."

I hesitated. I stopped breathing.

"I'm staying with her. There are the children and it's the right thing to do. I just can't leave her."

A voice came out of me that was so clear and deep that it gave me pause. I said, "Okay. Then I want a clean break. No more meetings, no more phone calls, no more anything. It's done."

We hugged, said goodbye, and he left. I closed the door behind him. It was over. I felt nothing. I was numb.

Two nights later, Lucas called and sobbing, he told me he made the biggest mistake in his life by leaving me. I was tempted but kept my resolve. He kept on calling, begging for me to return. It killed me but I said no.

I swore I'd never do that again. I pled temporary insanity. I was crazy, crazy in love, crazy with passion. So crazy I couldn't and wouldn't think straight.

I asked my latest longtime shrink, Bob, a question afterwards, "Bob, can you promise me I'll never do that again?"

He looked at me soothingly for a moment and said, "I can't promise that, Bob, I can't promise that."

I jokingly responded, "Then why am I paying you?"

I knew full well that it was my call, not his. It always comes back to me.

I run my life.

Shit.

Chapter Fourteen
Coming Out

The Fourth of July weekend was over. I came into town from Fire Island Pines. The family barbecue had moved to Ted and his wife Gloria's, a few blocks away from my parents' home in Brooklyn. My sister-in-law, Gloria, had known me since I was eight; we adored each other from day one. She was eighteen when she was dating my oldest brother, Ted, who was stationed in Korea. While he was away, Gloria would take my cousin, Rob, and me each Tuesday night to Coney Island in July and August to watch the fireworks, go on rides, and finally get a pistachio, soft ice-cream. She would pick us up in her car for a day at Riis Park to ride the furious waves. After she and Ted got married, they would take us to Radio City Hall to see a movie like *I'll Cry Tomorrow,* which had a stage show with the Rockettes. I knew this was all at Gloria's instigation because my brother, Ted, never took me anywhere before she arrived. As the years rolled by, Gloria and I would talk and talk, spending hours talking over a cup of coffee after my brother and the kids had gone to bed. We always had one more thing to say. The family barbecue was always a blast; family, friends, great food, and wine, and much hilarity and carrying on. But now, it was July 6th, the Monday after. Everyone went home and I was going to return to the Island the next day but not before I took care of some business. I called Sadie and Frank and said I'd like to come over. I had something to tell them. Sadie asked what. I said that I'd tell them in person. I had decided to come out to my parents.

I arrived at the house at 11 a.m. Sadie put out some coffee and asked if I wanted something to eat. I said no. My father was already sitting at the kitchen table, the center of the house, reading the Daily News. I asked Sadie to sit down, too; she was always fussing about the sink or stove washing a stray dish or preparing the next meal. She sat down.

"What's the matter?" Sadie asked.

"I have something I want to tell the two of you and it's hard for me to say it, but I want to say it."

My father put the paper down and sat quietly, expectantly in silence.

Sadie asked, "What is it? You seem so serious."

"Well, I have something to tell you... Something I haven't told you and now need to tell you."

"What is it, Rob?" my dad asked.

Tears welling up in my eyes, I said, "Well, here it is. I'm gay."

I stopped breathing. I looked at them, first my mother and then my father.

Sadie broke the silence, "I don't believe it. You were living with Ana and then there was Sarah and Jan. I don't believe it."

What made me think that she did believe it was the hardly detectable smile at the corner of the right side of her mouth, which betrayed what she was saying. Maybe she remembered I was always talking about my classmate Johnny in the second grade. Maybe she recalled that I was the head of the James Dean club in Junior High and got into trouble because I organized my class to wear black on the first anniversary of his death in 1956. Maybe it was because I didn't have so many girlfriends in high school. Maybe it was because I became obsessed with *West Side Story* and went to the theatre all the time in between football practices. Maybe she remembered how close I was to my seminary buddy, Sean.

"Ma, it's true. I like men. I always have."

"What happened? How did this happen?" Sadie asked.

I replied, "Nothing happened. I'm just gay and tired of pretending I'm not."

My father was silent. It killed me. What was he thinking?

"Dad," I implored, "Say something. Please."

A full thirty seconds dragged on. He was gathering his thoughts. He was a man of few words. He finally spoke.

"Robert, you are my son and I love you. That's it. I love you."

My eyes moistened.

"Thanks, Dad. Thanks."

Sadie got up and started to move about. She picked up a piece of cheesecloth and started to dust the kitchen blinds. She needed to open the window.

She looked over at me and with the devil in her eye, asked, "You can open the window, right? It's not too strenuous for you, is it?"

"Sadie, don't be a wiseass. I'll open your window."

"Does this mean you're never going to wash the outside windows in the porch? You know, the ladder is heavy."

"Sadie, cut it out. I'll do your windows."

The morning moved on. I told Sadie and Frank I wanted to tell each of my brothers, my sisters-in-laws, my seven nieces and nephews. Today. I was ready to go on my mission. So, I gave my mother and father a hug and a kiss and said I loved them. But Sadie had one last plea.

"Robert, make a mother happy."

"What, Ma?"

"Sleep with boys *and* girls."

I laughed out loud and so did Frank, rolling his eyes as he uttered, "My wife, my wife…"

The hard part was over. The next day I went to the house in Fire Island Pines and fell into a funk. Something died in me. It was who I used to be, the one living two lives. I was this singular, newer version of myself, the latest edition. It was going to take some getting used to. So I stayed in the pool, in the glorious sun, with my gay housemates, and just allowed the feelings to surface.

Sadie turned seventy-one on July 21st. We all went over to the house, had a cake, and sang "Happy Birthday." Afterwards, when everyone went home, my dad excused himself. We hugged, kissed, said we loved each other; he went downstairs to do something or other. I was alone with Sadie in the kitchen. I helped her clean up. I asked how she was doing with all what I told her.

She looked down and said, "I'm having a hard time with it."

I said, "I'm sorry, Mom. I'm sorry. I know it's hard."

When the last dish was washed, dried, put away, I kissed her on the cheek and said, "I love you, Mom, and I'll see you."

I walked over to my car, drove to the city, parked the car, got into the elevator at 205 West 13thth Street, got off on the sixth floor, unlocked my apartment door, closed it behind me, turned on the light on the nightstand, and lay down on the couch. I looked up at the ceiling and stared. I had no words for what I was feeling.

After I came out to my parents on that Monday after the Fourth of July, I visited each of my three brothers and their families and told them as well. It went well except for one nephew, Tom, age 16, who couldn't look me in the eye. It killed me. Eventually, as time passed, he realized I was the same Uncle Bob he always knew and loved. I was relieved.

When I told Aunt Angie who had just come home from work, she asked me, "Is my son one, too?"

"You have to ask your son that, Aunt Ang."

And she did. And she did again. And again. And yet again.

My cousin, Rob, told me, "I think I came out to my mother ten times."

We laughed and thought it in character, not realizing that maybe something was wrong. Our family was replete with characters that were obviously not normal. We were living with mental patients. So was everybody on the block. So, who gave it a second thought? I would say to my cousin, Rob, "Given our parents, particularly Sadie and Angie, it's a wonder that we can buy a token, insert it into the turnstile, and get on a subway!"

Chapter Fifteen
Learning About Loss

After the exhilaration of coming out, my life took on a more somber tone; I started losing people I loved. In one case, it was the inevitability of old age and death, but in the other, it was the tragic loss of a generation of young people.

Aunt Angie was always well dressed, always went to work, and was entertaining and sociable. She often babysat for Gloria's two youngest, Tom and Krys, when they came home from P.S. 177. Gloria was working. Gloria would drive Aunt Angie home when Ted arrived. She would say the same thing each and every day.

"The kids came home from school. I gave them milk and cookies. They did their homework and then went out to play where I could see them. They behaved very well."

Gloria thought nothing of the repetitiveness of her daily description. It was Aunt Angie and she was just being herself. She didn't think anything was wrong.

As time passed, Aunt Angie showed more obvious signs of cognitive decline. She would keep all her lipsticks in the refrigerator, which in itself is not unusual, but she *never* did that before. Instead of storing ice-cream in the freezer, she placed it in the refrigerator door. She placed eight glasses of water on the first refrigerator shelf. On the second shelf, she positioned six slices of American cheese. One time, she almost caused a fire by placing newspapers too close to the range top. From that point on, the gas was shut off.

Her son, Rob, worked at N.Y.U./Bellevue as a hospital administrator and asked his boss and close doctor friend, Angelo Ferraro, to assess her.

"How is she, Angelo?" Sadie asked.

"Not good, Sadie. We need to do further tests. I'll give her son a referral where she can take a brain scan."

"Is my sister going to have to be put away?" she asked, hoping the inevitable wasn't so.

"I think so, Sadie, I think so."

My mother sat there in silence.

A day or two later in February 1983, in the middle of another snowstorm, Sadie who lived downstairs called up to her sister as usual and asked, "Angie, are you up?"

No answer.

Louder, "Angie, are you awake?"

"Yes, yes. But I can't get up from bed." Sadie, frightened, called her son who called me and we met at the house in Gravesend where we grew up. We spoke with Sadie briefly and went upstairs to see what was going on with Angie.

"Hi, Mom. Aunt Sadie says you can't get out of bed."

"I can't."

"Maybe we can help you, Aunt Angie."

It was clear that this was a turning point, a moment of truth. From this moment on, reality, as we knew it, was rapidly changing.

Robert went into the kitchen and picked up the wall phone receiver and dialed Dr. Gravano, the neurologist Angelo recommended at St. Vincent's Hospital in Staten Island. He made an appointment for that day.

We had to get her there so we both lifted Angie forward, turned her around on the bed, so that she was in a sitting position. She was in her nightgown and we had to put her in street clothes. We took off her gown, which was embarrassing for us, and we had to completely dress her from head to foot. What made us uneasy didn't seem to faze Angie. She was smiling and even laughing; in fact, adorable in the way only Angie could be.

A half-hour later, we had her fully assembled with overcoat and kerchief. The next task seemed overwhelming. Angie had forgotten how to walk across the room. Her son held her from behind, and I moved her feet in high heels one at a time, one in front of the other.

She would laugh out loud and say, "This is really something!" and laugh out loud again. We only loved her more.

"Okay, Aunt Angie."

I said to my cousin, "Let's get her to the head of the stairs."

Now we had to get her down these stairs and into the car. It seemed an impossible task. Step by step, all fourteen of them we lifted one foot to the next step and then the other foot to the same level. At each landing, Angie would chuckle a most infectious giggle. It seemed that she was amused that she forgot how to climb down the stairs.

Sadie came to the front door, "Angie, it's good. You're going to the doctor."

Angie just smiled. She went inside and watched us bring her sister down the outdoor steps and into the car.

Sadie, agoraphobic, waved goodbye, sadly, almost admitting the unthinkable; that she would never see her sister again.

Angie and Sadie had a cousin, Angela Papa, who lived around the corner. She wanted to be with us. We picked her up.

Angela was another family character, the only one of her contemporaries to go to college. She was pre-med originally but fainted at the sight of blood. She majored in biological sciences at Columbia University, where she earned her undergraduate and graduate degrees. Angela was our brilliant family member, yet she *was* eccentric. She walked as if in a race. She was very talkative and expressive. She was a health nut and really was ahead of her time. She took a myriad of supplements and urged others to do likewise. She ingested cloves of garlic by the bulb, which offended our olfactory faculties! All in the name of good health. It must have worked; she lived past 100, albeit with dementia.

Angela, who lived on the next block, was devoted to her two first cousins, Angie and Sadie. She visited them every day, had a cup of tea, left a newspaper, and then went on her way only to return if either needed something from Peluso's grocery on the corner.

We picked up Angela and got on the Belt Parkway, crossed over the Verrazano, and arrived at Dr. Gravano's office at 2:45.

"Hello, Angie, I'm Dr. Gravano."

He had a gentle manner; he was kind.

"Hello, Doctor," she smiled.

He took her inside and checked her vitals and then informed us that he would perform an M.R.I. Afterwards, we went into see Angie.

"How did it go, Mom?"

"He's a lovely man, but *who* is he?"

After looking at the results of the M.R.I., Dr. Gravano said Angie should be admitted to St. Vincent's Hospital that very day. Further tests were necessary to determine a full diagnosis. We thanked him for his input and were happy that he would be the attending physician. We drove off to the hospital.

We entered the E.R., which had been notified that we would be coming. Angie and Angela, who was dressed in a black kerchief with black earmuffs and a black topcoat over black slacks, sat opposite each other. The nurse looking at the two women asked, "*Who's* the patient?"

We almost laughed because to an outsider one couldn't quite tell.

Robert pointed to Angie and said, "My mother *here* is the patient."

The nurse took Angie inside to admit her. Robert was with them.

Angie stayed in St. Vincent's through the winter and spring. It had been determined that she had an inoperable brain tumor. She was agitated and sometimes had to be tied down for her own safety. She became mostly non-verbal. A nurse told her son she sometimes appeared frightened.

"She cries for her mother."

One time, I visited her and she was clearly out of it. I had my Walkman and asked her if she'd like to hear some music. I placed one earphone in her right ear and Aretha was singing out. Angie, in her famous Mae West persona, clicked her fingers to the beat and uttered, "Mmmm, mmmm. Oh yeah." For a flash, the Aunt I knew was present. She soon faded away.

One time, a priest asked her, "Angela, would you like to receive communion?"

"Well," she paused, "I don't know. I have to cook dinner."

He moved on.

On Mother's Day, Robert visited Angie who exclaimed, "Oh, it's my son!"

Rob smiled.

At the end of June, a bed opened up at Seaview Hospital and Home on Staten Island. She was moved to accommodations that were pleasant and inviting. It had a huge campus with a cheerful staff.

On Tuesday, July 12th, Rob boarded the Staten Island Ferry and took a bus to the nursing home. It was a sun-filled, blue-sky kind of day. He went to her room; she was already in her wheelchair.

"Mom, would you like to go outside?" No response. He placed his light briefcase on her lap and off they went.

"It's a beautiful day, isn't it, Mom?" Angie looked straight ahead.

Rob noticed that his mother had her legs crossed at the ankles, the way she always did. He recalled a photo of his mother as a child. In it, her legs were crossed in the very same way. From that moment to this, there was still something of who she was that still persisted. He was happy for that little trace that she was still here.

The son brought his mother back to her room. He bent down and kissed her.

"Goodbye, Mom, I love you."

He lowered his cheek and pressed it against her lips pretending she understood the moment. Maybe she did.

He left the room after a brief glance backwards and headed home.

The next day, I came home around six p.m. It was July 13th. My answering machine was blinking; I had two messages from my cousin.

5:30 p.m.

"Rob, I just got call from Dr. Gravano. He told me I should come to the hospital, my mother's not doing well."

5:34 p.m.

"Rob, I just got another call from Dr. Gravano. She's dead."

My cousin thought the first call was to prepare him for what was expected. The second call nailed it.

It was a traditional Italian three-day wake. My cousin wanted no embalming, no hideous make-up, no *special* dress. He chose a simple shroud in a pinewood casket, a closed casket. The burial took place at Calvary Cemetery in Woodside, Queens under the Kosciusko Bridge. There's something about a death in the family that makes you step out of your life and forces you to ponder what life is all about. I remember being stoic at the news of my beloved Aunt's death, even through the wake. It was at the burial, when they lowered the casket into the ground, that I lost it. I just wept and wept and wept. My pal of an aunt had died, and I was devastated.

Each year on July 13th, I play some Gregorian chant and remain in deep silence. Then I have a vodka Gibson and celebrate our time together.

Raising my glass high, "Here's to you, Aunt Angie! I love you. I miss you."

Russian Roulette

I spent four summers in Fire Island Pines from 1979-1982. As time passed, I heard that one of my housemates died, and then another, and then another.

These were men I ate with, went to Tea Dance with, hung out at the pool with, and joked around with. I read that a "rare cancer" was affecting some gay men. The symptoms were purple spots on their bodies and swollen nymph nodes. Many were dying. Some friends of friends had a strange pneumonia, pneumocystis carinii, that I never heard of before. The Christian Right called it the *gay plague*. Eventually it was named H.I.V./A.I.D.S. No one knew much about it since only gay publications like *The New York Native* and *The Advocate* covered it.

In the summer of 1982, I took an H.I.V. test with my own internist and waited days for the results. I was in my living room sitting in a high back Captain's chair when I got the call.

"Bob, I have good news. You're H.I.V. negative."

I got off the phone and sat there in silence as tears streamed down my face. I didn't realize how much the epidemic had affected me. I was relieved even though I didn't know I was harboring such dread. I was so grateful, that I determined to be safe in subsequent sexual encounters.

I'd been in denial. I'd been going from one romance to another and even made occasional visits to gay bathhouses. I was cautious in my public promiscuity; recreational anal sex was off the table in bathhouses, but not in romances. Apparently, I went out with gay men who weren't ill.

Sex those days was like playing Russian Roulette. It was a very, very dangerous game. I was one of the lucky ones.

In September 1982, after a breakup with Lucas, I started my doctoral studies at Yeshiva University and decided I would dedicate myself totally to my coursework, my research, and my full-time job. I had no time for socializing. Every moment was accounted for. There was no time for fun, and certainly no time for sex. There's no safer sex than *not* having sex.

Chapter Sixteen

Teacher, Counselor

I loved teaching at Fort Hamilton High School in the Bay Ridge section of Brooklyn. It was great fun. I was the only Latin teacher and taught all five classes. We would sing conjugations to Paul McCartney melodies like *Pono, ponis, ponit, ponimus, ponitis, ponunt, ponunt,* which could be sung to *Michelle.* I often had a class recite declensions as they were high school cheers. I also encouraged teens to greet me in Latin when we met in the hallways.

"*Salvē, Magister!*"

I would return their hello, "*Salvē,* Fares!" or, "*Ave,* Anna!"

They were encouraged to declare that though a dead language, Latin was alive and well at Fort Hamilton High. They shouted out to me, "*Latina vivit, Magister!*"

I wanted learning Latin to be fun. Latin is filled with thousands of conjugations in many tenses and voices and nouns and pronouns in lots of cases in three genders; masculine, feminine, and neuter. A lot of the learning was rote. After all, *"Repetitio est mater studiorum."* Or, "Repetition is the mother of all learning." So, how to make repetition fun?

We were reviewing the demonstrative adjective this as is *this* man, *this* woman. In Latin, this has forms in singular and plural, five different case usages, and in all, three genders.

Here are the forms.

Cases	Masculine	Feminine	Neuter	[singular forms]
Subject	*hic*	*haec*	*hoc*	
Possessive	*huius*	*huius*	*huius*	
Indirect Object	*huic*	*huic*	*huic*	
Direct Object	*hunc*	*hanc*	*hoc*	
By, with, from	*hoc*	*hac*	*hoc*	

hi	*hae*	*haec*	[plural forms]
horum	*harum*	*horum*	
his	*his*	*his*	
hos	*has*	*haec*	
his	*his*	*his*	

The forms were printed on the black board and we recited them aloud to get the feel of the forms. Then I opened both doors in the classroom and said, "I want you to shout these forms as a cheer, as loud as you can, and you'll see what the result will be."

I had my pointer in hand and said, "1-2-3 Go!" At the top of their lungs that shouted, *"Hic, haec, hoc, huius, huius, huius, huic, huic, huic..."* and as they rounded to the next set of forms, all of a sudden, you could hear doors slamming from the other foreign languages classrooms.

At the end of the repetitive chorus, I instructed two students to close our classroom doors and said, "Job well done! Mission accomplished."

The U.F.T. teacher's strike had been going on since May 1968. It went on through November, accumulating 36 days of non-instruction. During this confrontation between the new community-controlled school board in the largely black Ocean-Hill Brownsville section of Brooklyn and the United Federation of Teachers, racial tensions between blacks and Jews increased.

It was the beginning of my third year of teaching Latin. I asked one of my brightest and favorite Latin students, Lesley, to meet with me after our staff picketed. I asked her to gather some of her classmates in her Latin second year class. I was concerned because they had a Regents exam at the end of June and they were missing instruction.

Lesley enlisted ten students together. We had a meeting on the bleachers of the football field.

"I'd like you to ask your parents if we can meet in your homes to study Latin."

"I know my parents will be fine with it," Lesley said. She lived in Bay Ridge.

"I'll ask my mom. I'm sure she'll say yes," Tameka said. She lived in the Farragut Housing Projects.

After a couple of days, we set up a schedule and met weekly. We called our renegade class *The Latin Freedom School.*

I never had a discipline problem. One term, I was in charge of study hall in the school auditorium at Fort Hamilton High School. There was a 17-year-old girl in the back who wore too much makeup, a dress that was much too tight, and too frizzy hair that towered high above her face. To complete the picture, she was chewing gum ravenously and was having a loud conversation with her girlfriend in a silent study hall. I went over to address this infraction of the rules.

"Be quiet, get rid of the gum, and take out a book!" I said.

She looked up at me with a sneer and said, "I gotta pee."

I said, "Cross your legs!"

Her jaw dropped, her eyes widened. She took out a book.

The Bay Ridge section of Brooklyn where I taught was a conservative neighborhood, the only district that voted for Barry Goldwater in 1964. I worked there in the era of L.S.D., school strikes, bussed in kids from the projects, kids living in communes, and the Civil Rights Movement. I was a fairly conservative young guy and to a certain point, I believed in decorum in the classroom.

I was out one Tuesday and upon my return the next day, I was in front of my Latin second year class. The attendance sheet that the kids signed the day before was on my desk in my Delaney book. I read the signatures and was filled with consternation.

Pulling the sheet out in front of me, I began to read the roll.

I inquired out loud, "Who's *Dick Hertz*?"

Little Marisa's jaw dropped.

Then, "Who's *Connie Lingus*?"

Jimmy looked down at his desk and turned red.

Finally, I enunciated, "Who's *Mike Hunt*?"

The class shifted uncomfortably in their seats.

After a moment of class uneasiness, I looked out and slowly said, "I am very disappointed in this class. Very disappointed."

Never happened again.

I also taught French first year at Fort Hamilton High School in the early 1970s. It was the first day of the fall term and I was orienting the students to the rigors of starting a new foreign language. Everything was going along well, but this kid in the back of the room kept on talking while I was.

I looked at his Delaney Card and said, "Johnny, be quiet!"

He mumbled something rude and I said, "Cut it out! Don't pull that nonsense here, ever!"

I looked him straight in the eye until he looked down in submission to my authority. I then stared out the window in a feigned appearance of disbelief to cement the moment.

Well, Johnny complied and was never rude again in my classroom. As a matter of fact, he never returned. Won the battle, lost the war.

One semester, I was the teacher-in-charge of the emergency room; it was what passed as a nurse's office at Fort Hamilton High School. It was two adjoining rooms, one for the girls and one for the boys. The nurse's aide was Ms. White, who was black. She and I handled students in need of a Band-Aid or a cot due to nausea. If medical services were necessary, we had connections with the local hospital.

It was now the mid-1970s and the Civil Rights Movement was in full swing and for a while, a long while, we, white teachers, were routinely disrespected by black teens whom we didn't know. A few years earlier, I remembered stopping a black girl for some infringement.

I said, "Stop yelling in the halls, young lady!" as I grabbed her arm.

She retorted, "Go fuck yourself and get your hands off me!"

It became clear to me that we, a predominantly white staff, had lost control of a large segment of the student body. If a teacher had sway with a student, that insolence would never occur. It was those we didn't know who felt at liberty to be contemptuous of our authority.

One day in the emergency room, while Ms. White was next door, I was sitting at a desk in the back of the boys' room. I was looking over medical records when a tall, lanky, young, black teenager entered the doorway; he made use of the mirror on the wall. We were twenty feet apart.

Arranging his fedora this way and that, he finally had it just the way he wanted when he saw I was watching him. Turning around a full 180 degrees, he scoffed at me saying, "What you lookin' at?"

Looking him straight in the eye, I said matter-of-factly, "Nothin' much."

His tough-guy exterior disintegrated into a laugh. He said, "Yo, man, *that's funny!*"

From that day forward whenever we ran into each other in the halls, he would greet me with a huge smile and say, "Mr. S, you the bes'"

Often I would see students that I knew laughing and rollicking in between classes and I would confront them.

"*What's going on here*? We must be doing something wrong. You're having too much fun!"

*

After years of trying to secure an appointment as a guidance counselor, I finally transferred to Christopher Columbus High School in the Bronx in October 1980. It was a dream job and I loved what I was doing.

Before I left Fort Hamilton High, some kids in a psych class I was teaching gave me a good-bye card. At the time, we were studying the nature of love. There are times when I go into darkness and forget who I am or who I was. One such time I found that card and read the following from my student Ki Hwan, "What is love? I still don't know what it is, but I think I loved you, Mr. Scherma."

In an instant, darkness turned to light.

*

Richard

Every once in a while, a special student appears before me. From the first moment I met him, I knew I would be a significant part of his life and he would be a part of mine. Over the years, I consider him the son I never had, my Jamaican son.

Richard entered Columbus High School as a sophomore in the 1994 from his native Jamaica. He was placed in the math/science program for our brighter students and I was his counselor. He had a smile that lit up his face and a personality to match. Soon, he became a fixture in my guidance office and worked for me during his lunch hour. We got to talking.

"I live with my dad in Harlem and it's not easy. We fight a lot and don't get along," Richard explained. "My mother lives in Jamaica and hasn't got the means to take care of me."

Although he lived in Manhattan, he gave the Bronx address of his aunt who lived across the street from Columbus.

His sophomore year passed without incident; he joined the track team and got into several advanced placement classes which earned him future college credit.

Right before holiday break in December of his junior year, I asked, "Hey, Rich, what are you doing during Christmas?"

"Nothing much. I'm going to be with my father and that's no fun."

When we returned to school in January, I asked, "How was Christmas?"

"Horrible."

"What do you mean?"

"Dad and I got into a row and we fought. It even got physical. I called the cops. They came and separated us and took me to social services."

"Richard, what then?"

"I told them my story and that *I was not leaving* until they found a place for me to live! I sat there on a wooden bench and didn't budge."

"So, what happened?"

"They saw that I meant it and that night they found a group home here in the Bronx, near the school."

"Richard, good work! You're amazing."

"I just had to do something. I couldn't stand it anymore."

The group home had several boys who came from similar circumstances of negligence and/or abuse. While Richard shared their backgrounds, he knew that education was the way out and forward. He had enough street smarts to not show that he was a nerd, but the staff realized he was bright and eventually gave him his own room, so he could study without distraction. He stayed away from the home as much as he could because of the track team, which practiced every day and had meets on Saturdays.

As the years passed by, Richard became more and more popular in school and maintained a high average. His group home became a safe haven for his studies. Still there was tension because of the special treatment he was getting.

It was now senior year. One day he came to the office with bandages on his head and bruises on his face.

"Richard, what happened?"

He sat in his usual chair, sighed, and said, "A few weeks ago, this new guy came into the home and he started to ride me. We took it outside. I beat his ass in front of everybody. He was 6'3" and I was 5'9". He was humiliated. I didn't care. I just had to show him he couldn't push me around."

"Yesterday, when I got home, I picked up my mail and went up to my room. I got an acceptance package from Syracuse University. As I opened my door, he blindsided me with a hammer to my head. I beat his ass again and home staff took us to the local precinct. We had blood all over us."

"They took him out of the home and placed him elsewhere. I didn't press charges and was happy that in summer I'd be in Syracuse starting a new life."

Richard looked sullen and incredulous. He just wanted to study and graduate and go to college.

"Why is life so hard, Doc?"

"I don't know, Rich, I just don't know. You just keep moving forward, one step at a time. If you need to rest and nurse your wounds, do so. You and I will continue talking over the years and you'll tell me all about it. Then back to the books."

I had one more job to do.

Richard was undocumented. He made Columbia but didn't have a green card at the time of his acceptance. I got him over to The Door, an organization in SoHo with a plethora of services for teens. We found a lawyer, David, a godsend, who got him on the path to becoming a citizen. I went down with the lawyer to the immigration department and witnessed the conferral of his green card in late August. He was on his way to citizenship, which he achieved five years later. But now it was high school graduation, with a future that looked promising. He was going to Syracuse University in the fall. I took him out to celebrate at Pete's Tavern in the city.

It was now the day after graduation when the kids return their caps and gowns and get their report cards. I met him at the front door. I gave him a card with some cash, which I knew he needed.

"Doc, thanks, I'm going to miss you."

"We'll always be in touch, Richard. Besides, I'm looking forward to the day you graduate from Syracuse!"

He looked sad and detached as he left the building, his counselor, his friends, and his recent life.

A month later, he was getting ready for college. He needed a few things; I made sure he got them. We wrote and spoke for the next four years.

Then it was time for college graduation. I flew up to Syracuse and saw him get his degree in finances. This was the second graduation of his I attended in person.

Syracuse University

His father was present and I couldn't help but feel perturbed around him. However, he and Richard had a rapprochement and that superseded my feelings. Forgiveness is good for the soul.

A terrible thing happened six years later. His dad was mugged in Harlem and murdered. Three months later, Richard's grandmother died. Richard was devastated. He had been working for a corporate financial firm in Connecticut and just couldn't do it anymore. His bereavement caused him to leave his job. His best friend, Kevin, told him come to Atlanta and heal. Six months later, he found a new job at G.E.

Now it was time for the next hurdle. Richard applied to M.I.T. for an M.B.A. program and got in! He needed a loan and I co-signed for it. Two years later, he graduated and, of course, I attended that graduation as well. The young teen I first met at fourteen years of age was now a full-grown adult with work experience and an M.B.A. from M.I.T.

M.I.T.

I was proud to have attended his three graduations, the only one on the planet to do so.

He was the son I never had, *my* Jamaican son. He is essential to my life. While he was growing up, I just made sure to be around him to encourage him when he needed it and help him keep on course. In psychotherapy, we look to see if the patient has the essential quality of *resilience*. Can you take the hard knocks that life most assuredly sends your way? From the start, I knew Richard was resilient. Life wasn't going to crush him. He was a survivor. I simply helped him along. It is clear to me that *he* made his life a success. He continues to do so.

We're still in touch via phone or FaceTime or email or texting. When he comes to New York, we meet for dinner or a glass of wine. He is now 40 as he just moved to Nairobi, Kenya, continuing his financial career. One day, he wants to have his own company. I am certain he will make it happen.

Chapter Seventeen
The Love of My Life

I told my friends I wasn't ready. Although I had just earned my doctorate in June, I still had to sit for the New York State psych licensing exam. I had too much on my mind to meet a new guy.

I sat for the exam the last Friday in October 1984 and was informed that the results would come in the mail the following spring. As early November rolled around, I notified my friends and family that I had started to jog again, had dropped ten pounds, and was now ready to start dating.

In November 1984, my sister-in-law, Gloria, was working in eldercare and touted me to this male nurse she knew; he wanted to meet me. His name was Kevin and we arranged to get together for a dinner. I was forty-one at the time and fit into my size 32 Levi's and had my curly locks. I discovered that this cute guy in front of me was thirty-two and was the type that took off his shirt and bared his chest at *The Saint* and other gay dance and sex halls. His short, blonde haircut, hazel eyes, and chiseled features only added to his fit appearance. He was hot and seemed intelligent to boot.

After dinner, we went to his apartment in the East Village.

"Hey, Bob, want some wine?"

"Sure."

"I'm gonna play some *Talking Heads,* do you mind?"

"Fine with me."

He played cuts from *Stop Making Sense* and started to dance. As I watched him, I got aroused.

He sat down next to me and we sipped wine and chatted. I listened intensely as he told me story after story of his life.

"Sometimes, as a nurse, you get really close to someone and you're rooting for him and one day you walk in and you find out he died after you saw him the night before. It's heartbreaking."

He told me more details of his childhood and his adult life. With the second glass of wine, he leaned towards me, and said,

"I feel like I've known you all my life."

The talk and laughter continued and we shared a kiss. When we parted that night, we said we'd call each other again.

When he *didn't* return my call, all I could mutter under my breath was, "*Men!*" He was a charmer in the same way my lover, Lucas, was; a thin veneer of allure, magic, and charisma with little depth and less authenticity. You didn't get the real person, but a glamorous representation of one. He did me a favor by not calling back.

"I feel like I've known you all my life."

Yeah, right.

In early December, my friend, Linda, said she had someone she wanted me to meet. His name was Beryl. They frequently bumped into each other at parties with friends they had in common and often had amiable conversations. He was also a good friend of Leda's, whom I met at Linda's fortieth birthday party in July. Leda and I enjoyed each other's company; we spent the entire evening chatting and amusing each other. And so, Linda and Leda thought that Beryl and I should meet; they seemed to enjoy playing matchmaker for two gay guys. Beryl had recently come out as gay at the *est* Six Day Training, an advanced personal growth course. Apparently, his friends already knew what he had finally admitted to himself. He was looking to meet someone. I told Linda to give him my number.

A few days later, on a Monday night, when I got back to the apartment, I saw the red blinking light on my answering machine. I pressed the play button and heard, "Hi Bob. My name is Beryl. Linda gave me your number and she and Leda want us to meet, so let's meet. Here's my number... I'll wait for your call and look forward to hearing from you."

His voice was deep and his enunciation was crisp and clear; he could have done voiceovers in commercials or been an F.M. radio announcer. I thought, *Sexy.*

Since it was past eleven, I called him the next evening. After making our introductions, I brought up something we had in common.

157

"I understand you did the *Six Day* as well as the *est* training."

"Yeah, the *Six Day* was phenomenal and powerful. Because of it, I came out," Beryl volunteered.

"So, you're a *homosexual*," I teased.

"Yep, queer as a three-dollar bill," Beryl chuckled. "When did you come out?"

"I did *est* seven years ago and it changed my life. I took a seminar a year later called *About Sex* and stood up and said to the crowd, 'My name is Bob and I'm going out with a woman I love, and I have all these gay feelings and I'm absolutely stuck.' By the next summer, I was out at Fire Island Pines."

Beryl then said, "I went to the *Six Day* with a beard and they insisted facial hair meant you were hiding. I agreed and so I shaved and became gay!"

We both laughed. I thought, *A sweet guy, talkative, personable.*

After a while, we agreed to meet for dinner the following Thursday night.

I was a little nervous as the next two days went by, but soon it was Thursday night and Beryl appeared at my door. He had very distinct features, with dark, close cut hair, and intense brown eyes that were enhanced by rounded wire-rimmed eyeglasses resting on a diminutive, yet sharp, nose. I noticed that his lips were thick and luscious and wondered how they would feel pressed against mine. His bookish face had a smile that disarmed me. A blue pinstriped shirt and blue jeans showed off his slender body, and penny loafers added to his casual, relaxed look.

After a few hearty hellos and nice-to-meet-you's, I asked him to please sit down and how about a glass of wine. For the next hour, there was non-stop conversation and laughter. We spoke about Linda, whom I worked with, and then about Leda and her husband, Michael, both of whom he knew from his days at Temple University. We talked about where we grew up, discovering that our backgrounds were very different. He was from Tamaqua, a small town in Pennsylvania, and I was from Brooklyn. We both came from big families, but his were scattered all across the country while my three brothers still lived in Brooklyn within a ten-block radius of my parents.

"How do you like having them all so close?" he asked me.

"My living in Manhattan makes it easy. I visit when I want and leave when it's *enough*. I like seeing my nieces and nephews, but my mother considered me an apostate when I migrated to the city without being married. Apparently, I was breaking many Italian-American bylaws."

Beryl looked amused.

I went on, "My mother, Sadie, didn't speak to me for a week when I told her I was moving to the city. A few years later, she told me, 'I moved out of the slums and *you* moved back!'"

We both laughed out loud.

I thought, *He's a good audience.*

"What about religion? Are you religious?" I asked.

Beryl chortled, "I studied to be a rabbi for six weeks before I realized I didn't believe in this stuff. I'm an atheist. I don't believe in God and I don't believe in an afterlife."

Undeterred, I declared, "Well, I was a religious kid, studied to be a priest for nearly four years, left the seminary, and became a fallen-away Catholic. I still believe in God and certainly believe in an afterlife."

I thought, *No common ground here.*

We had another glass of wine and Beryl, a smoker, asked if he could have a cigarette. I said sure. Somehow it didn't bother me that he smoked, even though I stopped fourteen years ago. All I could think of was that I wanted to touch the slight hint of hair on his chest that was exposed because the two top buttons of his shirt were opened.

The hour flew by and we were off to *Arnold's Turtle*, my favorite vegetarian restaurant on West 4th off Bank Street. Beryl had an array of veggies; asparagus, red bell pepper, onion, mushrooms, ginger, and garlic, stir-fried in peanut oil and garnished with toasted sesame seeds served over rice. I had a traditional-style vegan shepherd's pie. We both had tea. Beryl smoked away and the conversation was fast and easy. We liked each other's company. I wasn't sure if he liked vegetarian fare, though. He seemed to pick at his meal. I thought, *Maybe I should have picked another restaurant.*

By 11 o'clock, we ambled back toward my apartment house on West 13th Street. I turned to him and said, "Beryl, I'd like to get to know you. Why don't we meet again?"

"Absolutely. I'm going to this Christmas-tree decorating party Saturday night, why don't you join me?"

"I'd love to!"

He hopped in a cab home to Stuyvesant Town and I returned to my apartment. As I waited for the elevator, I thought, *I like this guy. I feel something could grow here. It's not wild passion; it's relaxed, slow, gentle.*

I knew I did from that first
moment we met.
It was…not love at first sight
exactly, but—familiarity.
Like, oh, hello, it's you.
It's going to be you.
Game over.

–Mhairi McFarlane

Beryl with Leda at Christmas party

At precisely 7:30 p.m., my buzzer rang. I thought, *Prompt! A man of his word.*

We walked over to Greenwich Street to the party; it was about a fifteen-minute walk. We took the elevator up to the fifth floor and entered a magnificent apartment. It had spacious rooms, an art gallery, and a view of the Hudson River. I thought, feeling a little inadequate, *And I live in a studio apartment!*

Beryl introduced me to our host and hostess who were most gracious as they welcomed us and took our overcoats. I thought, *An elegant crowd.* We then spotted Linda and Leda and hugged them hello. Linda smiled devilishly at me and gave me a sly and knowing look. I think I saw Leda give Beryl a wink. I was more at ease, but I needed a glass of wine, which I procured readily. Beryl bounced around the room and it was clear he was social and well liked. I thought, *He's presentable.*

The *hors d'oeuvres* came out, the champagne was poured, and the task at hand was clear; the boxes of ornaments were to the right, the Christmas tree was to the left. People started selecting ornaments and placing them on this branch and that. At one point, I picked up a red horse ornament with a white, cottony mane. I placed it on an interior branch. I turned to talk to someone and Beryl came by and looking at the red horse ornament said, "Who put this here? It doesn't belong *here*."

He removed it and placed it to the *right* location. I didn't say a word. I thought, *Very opinionated, likes to be right, a little bitchy.* I took another sip of my champagne.

The evening moved merrily along. There was much food, more drink, dancing, and general carrying on. The tree was fully decorated and people were now in small groups having intimate conversations. Soon it was 1:30 a.m. and people started to leave. At two a.m., Beryl and I decided to get going. As we approached West 13th Street, I asked nervously, "Beryl, would you like to come upstairs?"

Beryl gave a tentative, "Yes."

He was clearly a little anxious.

"Come on up, we'll have some Remy Martin."

"Great."

When we got to my apartment, I said, "Have a seat. I'll put on some music and I'll get the brandy and some glasses."

I selected several romantic Jean-Pierre Rampal LPs to set the mood and then got two snifters, poured some Remy, went over to the sofa, and gave Beryl his drink.

I hit his glass and said, "Happy Holidays!"

We smiled and took a sip.

"I really enjoyed seeing Leda again and her husband, Michael. I didn't know he worked as an art director for Woody Allen."

"Yeah, he also did a great film about Catholic school boys, *Heaven Help Us,* and *Moscow on the Hudson.* Robin Williams was in that one," Beryl offered.

"I also liked our host and hostess, very hospitable and friendly."

"Bob and Jeri are great. I used to work with Jeri in publishing."

"Thanks for inviting me. I'm glad we went."

Soon, we were both quiet.

I was sitting next to him and saw that we were at an impasse. I thought, *Who makes the first move?*

I felt he was apprehensive, maybe timid, and certainly vulnerable. I was less so; I leaned over and kissed him. He had the most luscious lips, thick and soft and it was clear; the man knew how to kiss. I thought, *I could make out with him for hours.* I started unbuttoning his shirt and liked his lean and hairy chest. My mouth devoured his upper body and then returned to those delicious lips again. He then started unbuttoning my shirt and touched my chest in a most tender yet purposeful way. While kissing, we kicked our pants and shoes and everything else to the side. We opened the Castro convertible and soon we let the games begin.

After making love, we lay there quietly and serenely. He asked, "Do you mind if I play?"

I said, "Sure," not knowing exactly what he meant.

He proceeded to touch and caress my body in a most gentle way. The playground was open, and I thought, *he and I are going to play a lot.*

We soon fell asleep in each other's arms.

Beryl and I had been going out for a few months when we spent a weekend with his parents in Allentown, Pennsylvania. His mom put us in the bedroom upstairs, the one with the double bed in it. As a couple, we were a hit. His dad, Joe, and his mom, Dorothy, welcomed us into their home, both their son and his lover. Joe was very bright, had who graduated high school at sixteen and entered college soon after. He was a jokester and would go for a laugh to a fault.

Dorothy was delightful. She and I got along from the get-go. Gentle, intelligent, attentive, she won my heart over with her flash of a smile.

Now, it was time for Sadie and Frank to meet Beryl. I decided to visit them and let them know what I was intending.

Another coffee around the kitchen table. Sadie, Frank, and me.

"I want you to meet somebody."

"Who?" asked Sadie.

"The man I'm seeing. His name is Beryl. I've already met his parents. I think it's time for you to meet him."

Sadie got up, went over to the sink, and declared, "I don't care what you do in your own life, but don't bring it into my house."

I recognized the line. It was from the televised version of that book *Consenting Adult* which opens with a letter from a college sophomore telling his parents he's gay. The parents are devastated. The *A.B.C. Sunday Night Movie* starred Martin Sheen and Marlo Thomas. When the son says he wants to bring home his boyfriend, Marlo Thomas used that *very* line.

I said, "Sadie, this isn't a television show. This is real life. You're going to meet him."

"No, I'm not. I don't want to meet him! Don't bring him here."

I asked her to sit down. *Now.*

She sat down. I looked her right in the eye. I spoke.

"Sadie, if you don't meet Beryl, you will *never* see me again."

We were standing over a widening abyss. She stopped a moment. She didn't speak. Then she did.

"Okay, I'll meet him."

Sadie always tried to push the envelope to have it her way. I was like her and she knew I'd push back, harder. When I wanted to join the Lafayette High School football team, she said no. I went to my dad, he signed the papers, and for three years, I was on the team. When I told her I wanted to be a priest, she gave me the silent treatment for a week. I went to the seminary. When I told her I wanted to move to the city, a no-no for an unmarried Italian son, she didn't talk to me for another week. I moved to the city and lived there for eighteen years. When I realized the truth about myself, I went over to the gay life and let her know. She knew I'd do what was important to me no matter what she said. I was her favorite; she wasn't going to jeopardize that.

My dad entered the conversation, "Sadie, it's *Rob and Beryl.* They're together." As he said this, he placed his two index fingers together to show two side by side. "We'll meet him."

Sadie, begrudgingly, "Yeah, we'll meet him."

"Great! I'm bringing him to Ron and Dorie's wedding. You'll meet him there."

Before I could hear a response, I said goodbye with a hug and a kiss and got the hell out of there.

My brother, Ron, was getting married for the second time; this time to Dorie. He wanted me to be his best man, again.

"Ron, are you *sure*? I was best man for your first marriage. That didn't last."

I was closest to Ron because we communed with each other from our hearts. We trusted one another. But Ron was impish and always causing havoc at family events. He was a kidder and a trickster and made us laugh out loud.

When I was pre-pubescent, Ron and I couldn't stand each other. But when I became a teen, we became a mutual admiration society. Even though I was still the kid brother, now as a teenager, I had my own thoughts and he engaged me in conversation and made it clear that really liked me.

Ron was a funny, bright, mischievous, and generous soul. We could talk about the things that were important to us; everything. We talked about love and life and future ambitions and music. He was the brother I felt most comfortable with. I could say anything to him and he could say anything to me. We really listened to each other and approved of each other as individuals. We were fellow seekers, finding our own truths. We saw each other's souls and we liked what we saw.

Ron

When I was twenty-five in 1968, Ron and I decided to jog a couple of times a week. We started at E.J. Korvettes Department Store on Shore Road and Bay Parkway and ran to the Verrazano Bridge. We felt like we climbed Mt. Everest when really, we only ran a mile. When we reached the bridge, we'd turn back, light up a cigarette, and walk back. And we'd talk.

One time, I remember telling him that I was bored with the four women I was dating and that I was going to drop them all. He advised, "Rob, maybe keep one of them around until you find someone you really like." An older, wiser brother advising a younger, greener kid brother. Ron was always happy to meet the important women in my life; we'd double date and triple date and quadruple date. He was always a part of my life.

When I was best man for Ron and Dorie, Ron was most welcoming to my new "friend" Beryl and my new lifestyle. He was even trying to hook me up at that wedding.

"You see that guy over there, I want you two to meet."

"Ron, I'm with Beryl. We're just starting out. We're getting serious."

"Okay, just thought I'd give you another option. Forget about it."

Ron was very accepting of my decision to be gay. I'll never forget that. Never. He was generous of spirit and was very welcoming to Beryl. He and Beryl got along well and we would often go out with him and Dorie.

Ron was a joker as far back as I could remember. Besides stabbing the container of Borden's milk in four spots so that the milk would be streaming out onto Sadie's kitchen table or the ritualistic stabbing of the Thanksgiving turkey, knowing Ronny, we would just laugh.

Sadie called out, "Ronny, Ronny, stop it, stop it!"

Forget it.

We would visit our Aunt Jo in the city. We'd be sitting around the table, one of those portable tables that opens up into a huge surface. Aunt Jo was a fabulous cook. However, Ron discovered a little screw that he could and would unscrew. The table would fall slowly onto our laps and my Uncle Vince would yell out, "Why does this always happen when my relatives come over and not yours? Call the man to fix it tomorrow! *Goddamnit!*"

Ron's wedding to Dorie was held at the former Russian embassy on the Upper East Side. Beryl was my date. A secularized rabbi performed the wedding ceremony and afterwards, we moved into the next room for the cocktail hour. Sadie and Frank were sitting with my Uncle Vince and Aunt Jo with Dorie's parents. I brought Beryl over.

"I'd like to introduce you to Beryl."

My father stood up and greeted Beryl holding his hand with two hands, one on top and the other.

"I'm very pleased to meet you, Beryl."

"Thank you, Mr. Scherma. I'm glad to meet you, too."

"Sadie, here's Beryl."

Sadie stayed in her chair, looked up, put out her hand, limp, and cracked a near smile that was bordering on a sneer.

She said, "Pleased to meet you."

My mother's younger brother, Uncle Vince, said to have been connected to that family that doesn't exist, to that *consigliore* who got gunned down in Umberto's Clam House on Mulberry Street, gave a polite hello. His wife, Aunt Jo, said, "How do you do?"

I pulled Beryl away from the battlefront and took him over to the line of people waiting to get some hot food. Lucky for us, we got behind Gloria. I introduced them.

Gloria had a lot to contend with concerning her own brood of four; my nieces and nephews whom I'd known since they were born. They sat together. Frank who was running around with a blond bombshell who owned a rhesus monkey, Doug who was sitting next to his born-again Christian wife, a refugee from the communists in Hungary, Tom who was cavorting with an older woman, a Newyorican, and Krystyne who was with her boyfriend, John, who was blacker than coal. Introducing Beryl to them would be a cinch.

"Glo, this is Beryl."

They exchanged warm hellos and pleasantries.

Gloria asked, "Did you meet Sadie and Frank?"

"Yes, I did."

"What was *that* like?" Gloria asked provocatively.

Beryl answered, "Well, Frank stood up, took my hand with *both* his hands, and said he was happy to meet me."

"And Sadie...?"

"Well, she gave me a limp hand and I think she sneered."

Gloria laughed out loud, "That's the best any of us got. Each of her daughters-in-law got the welcoming sneer the first time we met her. She doesn't like anyone taking her sons away from her. You got what we got."

I remember a conversation with my mother the day her third son, Ron, was getting married for the first time in 1962.

"When a son gets married, the mother goes one step down."

She acknowledged this fundamental truth and didn't like it.

Beryl, relieved, said, "I'll make her realize one day that she isn't losing a son, rather she's gaining another one."

We got our food, sat down, and I asked the waiter for another vodka Gibson up, no vermouth. Time for a breather.

Several months passed and Beryl and I would visit Sadie on a Sunday morning from time to time. One Sunday Sadie, Beryl [pronounced *Burl*] and I were having a cup of coffee at the kitchen table in Brooklyn. Sadie was telling us about her cousin Anita's husband, Willy, who wasn't the sharpest knife in the drawer.

"Willy is a dumb Hungarian!" she proclaimed.

I said, "*Ma,* Beryl is part *Hungarian.*"

Beryl, always the gentleman around the elderly, sat quietly, slightly perturbed but not showing it.

Sadie asked, "Who's Beryl?"

Now my mother couldn't get his name right for over a year and a half. She referred to him as Burl, which then became *Earl*. Another time Earl became *Oil*. Sometimes, *Herbie* and God knows why, *Dobie*.

I eyeballed her and nodded my head sideways toward Beryl and said, "*Beryl, Goddamnit!*"

Sadie, exasperated, asked, "What *kind* of name is *Beryl* anyway?"

Beryl, who hailed from the tribe of Judah, in his most somber baritone voice said, "I'm named after my dead grandfather."

Silence.

Now Sadie, who respected the dead more than the living, apologized profusely. From that day forward, she never forgot his name. She even affectionately called him *Berly-boy* on a subsequent visit.

And the word went forth. With a smile and a wink, everyone now referred to him as Berly-boy. He enjoyed it. Sadie had finally accepted him; he was on the inside now.

One time Beryl and I were talking about his mother, Dorothy.

"You always talk about Dorothy as if she's a perfect person, a saint."

"She is."

Coming from of a lifetime with Sadie who was no saint, had an opinion about everything I did, had no censor, and said whatever came into her mind, I knew most assuredly that parents *were* imperfect and had feet of clay like the rest of us.

"How can that be? Didn't Dorothy ever do something untoward?"

"No."

"Beryl, she can't be flawless. Can you come up with *one* complaint? I could give you a list of grievances against Sadie."

"Well, I can't. My mother was a good mother," he said, drowning in a sea of denial.

This was a typical conversation about psychological matters where he would assert, "Bob, things are just what they are. I'm not very introspective. I'm really quite shallow."

I asked myself what I was to do with this information?

I would say, "*Pshaw*. It can't be. You know, Socrates said the unexamined life isn't worth living."

He looked at me askance and said I insulted him.

I was living with a man these past six months who didn't look inward, not one iota. Here I was, studying at the Karen Horney Institute for Psychodynamic Psychotherapy after being steeped in Freudian theory in graduate school and years of therapy with more shrinks than I care to enumerate. Looking inward was my way of being in the world. Who was this man who didn't care to explore the inner journey, who just wanted the facts and would decide accordingly? He obviously was a *behaviorist* who didn't care how the first five years of life affected his daily living. I was appalled that I was apparently living with a *heathen*. I thought we had achieved a balance in our relationship; he was the *mind* in the relationship, I was the *heart*. He was the *atheist*, I was the *spiritual* one. He was the *witty* one with an acerbic tongue; I was the *funny* one who would choke if a harsh word crossed my lips. In some odd way, we complemented each other. *But not to believe in Freud!* Anyone with half a brain could see that in early childhood in order to maintain the love of those two towering figures, *our parents,* we had to do it *their* way and become a self that *they* approved of leaving behind who we truly were. Our true self has to be unearthed and liberated. But you needed to be conscious of these psychodynamics. I concluded that Beryl knew a lot about a lot, but when it came to self-examination, *he knew shit.*

I would tell him, "Beryl, you are the most *un-psychodynamic* person I know!"

He wore it like a badge of honor.

He would tell our friends, "Bob says I'm the most un-psychodynamic person he knows!"

I would retort, "Beryl, that's *not* something to be proud of."

He would then look at me and give me a broad wiseass grin. If he weren't so adorable in his ignorance, I would have thrown a pie in his face.

I Make A Shocking Discovery

It was 1988 and we were visiting Beryl's cousin, Kenny, who was a prosperous lawyer and owner of a soccer team that proved to be very profitable. Kenny was now retired at age thirty-nine and had a wife and three kids who lived in a new home they just built. It had *eight* bathrooms.

It was the day after Kenny's 13-year-old declared he was a man. The guests were in recovery from the *Bar Mitzvah* extravaganza of the night before and now it was Sunday brunch, time for a little nosh. The family out-of-towners assembled in the living room to do what we did best; eat. There was an array of bagels and lox, whitefish salad, blintzes, cheeses, chopped liver, miniature knishes, kugel, potato latkes, some *challah*; a little *hamentashen*, a huge seven-layer chocolate cake, and fresh fruit for the health-conscious. Coffee and tea were piping hot. After sampling practically everything and several cups of high-octane coffee, I had to make a trip to one of the eight lavatories. I was on the first floor, so I went to the main restroom facility.

This bathroom was quite lavish. It had a high-end commode accompanied by a bidet at its side. The whirlpool bathtub was neighbor to a corner steam shower. The vanity was wall-mounted and the fixtures complemented the contemporary look of this trendy bathroom. The problem was that the wall and floors had black tiles that were accented with shades of a tawdry pink. It looked like a bordello. What confirmed this impression was what I saw when I looked up. This enormous room had a mirrored ceiling.

I was stunned.

Then, I was aghast.

What I saw as I looked in the mirror was the beginning of a balding spot on the back of my head. I thought, *Am I losing my hair?*

Astonished and horrified, I shouted out for assistance, "Beryl! Beryl! Please come here!"

Again, "Beryl! Beryl! Please come here!"

I thought, *Where is that man?*

Alarmed, Beryl came running into the brothel and asked, "What's the matter? What happened?"

I pointed to the back of my head and the mirror above repeatedly and asked, "How long has *this* been going on?"

Calming down he said, "As long as I know you… Four years…"

Crestfallen and inconsolable, I sat on the commode or the bidet, I don't know which and mourned my fate.

"Bob, it's fine. Don't worry about it."

"Easy for you to say."

He left the bathroom and I closed the door behind him and set out to accomplish what I had resolved to do when I first entered this chamber of horrors.

When I stepped out into the crowd, I was a changed man. I wondered if I should wear a yarmulke from now on.

Ratner's

Beryl and I loved to go to Ratner's Delicatessen on the Lower East Side until 2002 when it closed. The New York Times called it a "kosher-dairy haven where rude waiters had dished out feather-light matzo balls and pucklike potato pancakes since 1905."

When you went there to dine, it was always a New York happening.

One Sunday afternoon, Beryl and I took the car into the city and got a parking spot right on Delancey Street in front of the deli. We walked in, got a table, took off our coats, and perused the menu. The fresh onion rolls were brought to the table, as were glasses of water. We made our decisions and called over the waiter who was very reminiscent of the comedic actor, Lou Jacobi. He was short in stature, a bit rotund, had a little black mustache, and was very serious about the task at hand.

He asked me, "What would you like, sir?" in a recognizable New York Jewish accent.

"I'd like some creamed spinach with two poached eggs, some *kasha varnishkes*. Oh, and a side of stuffed derma."

Our waiter beamed at me, "*Good choice!*"

Then he looked over to Beryl and asked, "And what would you like, sir?"

"I'd like to have lox and cream cheese with tomato and red onion on a *bagel.*"

"*Comes* with bagel!"

"*No,* on the menu it says you can have it with bagel or rye bread."

He was now speaking in clipped tones.

Again, "*Comes* with bagel!"

He looked at Beryl with disdain and sauntered away to fill the order. Beryl, feeling righteous, was annoyed because *anyone* could read on the menu that there was a choice between a bagel *and* rye bread. He was like a dog gnawing on a bone and holding onto it tightly.

"Beryl, let's just have a pleasant meal…" I implored.

"But he's *wrong!*" said Beryl, who had to be *right.*

Exasperated, I said, "Let it go, Beryl, let it go."

"I can't let it go!"

After a few moments, the waiter came back with our orders and placed them in front of us. He noticed that we had devoured the onion rolls and asked me, "Would you like some more onion rolls, sir?"

I said, "Yes, please."

In a few moments, more onion rolls came. The waiter was very pleasant and congenial to me but Beryl was getting the cold shoulder. Beryl was steaming mad, like a teakettle about to blow.

After we finished our luscious kosher delicacies, our waiter returned and removed our dishes and cutlery.

Upon his return, he asked me, "Would you like some coffee, sir?"

I said, "Yes, I'd like that."

He then nodded in Beryl's direction and asked me, "What about *him?*"

I turned to Beryl and asked, "Beryl, would you like some coffee?"

I didn't know what to do. I wasn't fast on the draw.

Fuming, he said, "*Yes!*"

I turned back to the waiter and said, "Yes, he would."

He walked away, almost in triumph, as we waited for what seemed an eternity for our coffee to arrive.

When the coffee did arrive, Beryl glared at the waiter. After the check came, Beryl said to me, "I don't want to tip him!"

"Beryl, we have to leave *something…*"

"Okay, but only 10%!"

He left the tip and I went to the cashier to pay the bill. We got out of there fast.

Next time when we had an urge for deli, we went to Barney Greengrass on the upper West Side.

Chapter Eighteen

I Miss My Dad

In his declining years, my Dad was hospitalized several times. Some strokes, some heart failure, general aging problems. I was the son who left work when I got the call and took him to the E.R. One day after a medical episode had subsided, we were sitting in a doctor's office for a final interview. However, the doctor, a woman with an icy demeanor said, "Let's schedule him for an M.R.I., a colorectal exam, a bone density scan, and a prostate cancer screening."

My dad leaned over to me, *"No more tests."*

I leaned over to this doctor and said, *"No more tests."* We left the hospital. No more tests.

I was always happy that I took my father to the hospital time after time. I felt I did all I could do for him. Our relationship was complete. Full. Overflowing. I loved the man, now eighty-six, and I knew he loved me.

It was mid-September 1990. My father had a stroke and was taken to Victory Memorial Hospital in Bay Ridge, Brooklyn. He was barely communicative but did seem to recognize us. He was very weak, had numbness on his face and arm and leg on the left side. His vision was compromised. He had loss of speech, had difficulty talking, and seemed to not fully comprehend what we were saying to him. His hospital physicians said it didn't look good.

I conferred with his primary care doctor and told him my father's wishes; do not resuscitate. My brother, Ted, spoke with him in another conversation and told him to do whatever was necessary to keep him alive. I was fuming at that, but it was too late. His primary care doctor did as Ted asked and ignored my father's request. My dad was put on life support.

Two weeks later, on September 29th, 1990, I was visiting my dad with Beryl and my cousin, Rob. He looked very pale and as if he were hanging on by a string. I kissed my dad on the forehead and said I'd see him in a day or two. We got in the car and drove back home. On the Brooklyn-Queens Expressway, I got a phone call. It was Ted.

"Dad just died. Come back."

Stunned and in shock, it hit me, *My father is dead.* Death, like love, came softly and almost as a surprise. In one moment, he was here. In the next, he was gone. How does one take in the loss of a parent? Who can articulate the consequences, the feelings, and the sense of loss bound up in this profound human event? Your life is changed forever, never to be the same. An archetypal figure disappears and you are looking as if into a void. Who can fill it? You learn the hard lesson, *no one can.*

One evening, maybe ten years later, I was driving home down Chambers Street after a long night at my practice. A song came on by Linda Ronstadt and James Ingram, *Somewhere Out There.* I could only think of my father. Perhaps he was thinking of me too and loving me somewhere out there.

Tears flowed down my face seemingly without end. I sobbed and lost my breath. It took me by surprise. I didn't know why this song on this night evoked such profound feelings. I just *missed* my dad, yearned to be with him. I was distraught until I got home to Beryl who loved my father so. He understood and held me close.

Chapter Nineteen

Sadie Finally Visits Stagnant Island

Sadie was agoraphobic and rarely ventured only a few steps outside our home in Gravesend. Granny, in her later years, became mentally unbalanced. She had paranoid episodes and plagued our neighbors with her mistrust and suspiciousness. Sadie stayed home to protect the homestead and keep a careful eye on her. Even after Granny died, Sadie's agoraphobia persisted. Once she ventured forth to the corner supermarket with her sister Angie and had a panic attack. She had her house, backyard, and front stoop. There Sadie felt safe.

Brooklyn home

A new world order was established as a result. The butcher delivered fresh meat and poultry every Saturday from Avenue S, as did the fish market vendor from Dahill Road on Fridays. The fruit and vegetable man came by on his truck right outside the house. The egg man brought six dozen eggs each Wednesday. The milkman came daily and soda man each week. The dry cleaner came each Thursday. If she needed her knives or scissors sharpened, a man with his grinding machine in a little pick-up truck arrived every few weeks. Sometimes Sadie needed to rid the house of unwanted items, the junk man came with his huge open truck, singing, "*Jink* man here, any ol' *jink*." Sadie had a doctor who came to her regularly to check her blood pressure; she even had a dentist who made house calls. Whatever else she needed, she had her sons.

My brother Mickey and his wife Delia had been inviting Sadie and Frank to come out to Staten Island for a holiday dinner. Year after year she would decline.

"Maybe next year, Mickey."

"Yeah, yeah," Mickey would sigh, defeated.

Mickey issued another invitation the year after Frank died.

"Ma, come for Easter dinner. Rob is coming with Beryl and so is cousin Rob. Why don't you come too? Say yes. Rob said he'd take you."

It was 1991, Mick and Delia had moved to Staten Island ten years earlier.

Sadie surprised Mickey when she said, "Okay, I'll come!" She could put it off no longer. She felt safe with her entourage. It was time to make the trek to Staten Island or as Brooklynites liked to call it, *Stagnant Island.*

Cousin Rob, Beryl and I arrived at Sadie's at 12:30 p.m. on Easter Sunday. It was a bit chilly but the heater in my 1985 Honda hatchback would warm the wintry air. Sadie needed assistance coming down the back stairs to the driveway and then to the car. Beryl and I lent our arms and shoulders to support her ample weight as she moved slowly to the front seat of the car. Cousin Rob grabbed the boxes of cannoli and the light, fluffy Italian cheesecake and headed to the back seat. Beryl assisted Sadie into the front seat but somehow when she landed, she was lopsided. Her line of vision was the inside of the car door nearest her.

"Ma, can we make you more comfortable. You're all bent over."

"No, no. It's all right. Let's get going."

"But, we can shift you a bit."

"It's *fine*. Let's go."

180

Beryl sat with my cousin in the rear and I backed out of the driveway and we were on our way to the Verrazano Bridge.

A few minutes away, heading toward Bay Parkway, Sadie inquired, "Are we on the bridge yet?"

"No, Ma. Not yet."

The radio was on and softly played Mariah Carey's *Someday* and then Bette Midler's *From a Distance.*

I entered the Belt Parkway; we were a mile away from the Verrazano.

"Are we on the bridge *yet?"* Sadie asked again.

"No, Ma, not yet."

A few moments later, we were on the ramp to the Verrazano Bridge and I said, "Ma, we're on the bridge!"

Straight away, "Can't you go any faster?"

At 1:30 p.m., we arrived at 99 Holly Avenue, our Staten Island destination. Mickey greeted us at the front door and he helped Sadie up the two stairs into the living room. Delia left the kitchen for a moment to say hello to everyone. We brought in the desserts and flowers and a bottle of bourbon and Limoncello and we headed downstairs where Mickey's two daughters, their spouses, and his granddaughter greeted us with great fanfare. It took Sadie a bit longer to get down the staircase, but with Mickey's assistance, she got seated at the table. Hugs and kisses and *how are yas*, then, "Where are the Manhattans?"

Mickey pointed to the bar where eight martini glasses were waiting. He pulled out a huge jigger of Manhattans and asked, "Who wants one?"

In a few minutes, we were all feeling just fine.

Then the food came out, a typical Scherma family feast. First, we had antipasto: bruschetta pizzaiola with mozzarella smoldering topped with cherry tomato halves, insalata caprese, thickly sliced tomatoes alternated with thick slices of mozzarella adorned with fresh basil and extra virgin olive oil, and some risotto croquettes. More Manhattans.

After a brief respite, it was the main events; first, linguini with red clam sauce, then veal cutlets Milanese, chicken cacciatore, and a fresh ham for the Americans in the crowd. Some sautéed asparagus, breaded and fried artichokes, and a fresh green salad were side dishes. Now the wine was pouring.

It was three hours in and it was time to go for a walk before dessert.

"Who's coming?" Mick asked. The men got up immediately, and after helping clear the table, we got our coats and went outside. Mick's granddaughter, Sabrina, joined us. The womenfolk stayed behind preparing the coffee, espresso, the dessert trays, and the after-dinner liqueur, Limoncello. It was a sunny yet chilly day, but a welcome relief to get the digestive process going.

We returned and had the cannolis and the cheesecake and some homemade biscotti that Delia made, a family favorite. There was also a blueberry pie, which called for some *Häagen Dazs* ice cream that was readily available. Warm beverages were served and now it was time to wind down with a sip of the traditional Limoncello. We were now all mellow.

An hour later, after much conversation and second servings, it was time to go. We helped clean up while Delia made take-home packages for each of us, including a second plate with desserts. We thanked her profusely and headed upstairs.

Mickey and I were in charge of Sadie's transport to the car. Mickey was at the top of the stairs. Sadie was at the bottom step and I was behind her. She gave me her cane and placed her two hands on the fourth step and proceeded to climb the stairs on all fours.

I looked up at Mickey and saw a bit of mischief in his eye. I said, "Mickey, don't."

He looked down and smiled an evil grin. Again, "Mickey, *don't!*"

Mickey couldn't restrain himself. As Sadie was climbing the stairs on all fours, Mickey went, "*Woof!*" I cracked up.

Sadie said, "Don't make fun of your mother. It's not right," as she continued up the stairs doggy-style.

We entered the car and headed back to Brooklyn. In the driveway, Beryl and I and Cousin Rob assisted Sadie to the back steps. She was having a hard time getting up the stairs in the dark. We turned on the back-porch light and kept the storm door ajar so we could maneuver her in.

"Beryl, help me with my left foot."

He put his shoulder into her left leg and somehow got the foot up the step. I was on the other side and with a concerted effort, we got Sadie into the house.

"Close the door! We'll get squirrels!" Sadie shouted in alarm. No squirrels joined us but a monstrous horsefly was buzzing about.

"Get out the Raid!"

She proceeded to spray the kitchen area so that we were choking and gasping for air. The fly disappeared into the haze and his corpse was found in the foyer.

"Ma, you got him!"

"Thank, God."

The fumigation settled and we could breathe again.

"Sadie, did you have a good time today?" Beryl asked.

"I did. It's good to go out, but it's better to get home."

Right before Thanksgiving in 1991, Delia, at age fifty-eight, succumbed to cancer after being diagnosed three months earlier. It was shocking. I believe Mickey never recovered from it. When he was with people, he was all laughs. When he was alone, he grieved.

One time, in the first year after Delia's death, we, brothers, took Mickey out for dinner. He had a second drink, maybe a third. He turned to me with a foreboding look.

"You've got to help me! You're a psychologist! You know better. I'm in great pain and I don't feel that you're helping me!"

I felt attacked at this stinging indictment. Was it true? Was I not present for him? Did I know how to be present to such pain?

I asked, gently, "What would you like me to do?"

I really didn't know what I could do.

He paused and in tears, said, "Be present. Be with me. I need you."

My older brother needed me, the kid brother. His broken heart broke mine.

I said, "Sure, Mickey, I'll be there. I'll be around. You'll see me, hear from me. I'll be there."

I resolved to telephone him often and make visits to Staten Island every month or so. We'd spend days together and just talk and laugh, you know, have fun. We were brothers who knew how to do that.

*

Beryl and I stopped at Dunkin' Donuts and bought a half dozen coconut covered donuts which Sadie loved at the moment. Frank had been gone these past three years. Today, fun was in the air, but I got serious for a moment. It was my birthday and turning fifty was freaking me out.

I turned to her and said, "Sadie, did you ever think that your youngest son would be sitting here telling you he was *turning fifty*?"

Leaning forward, at practically eighty-three, timing perfect, she asked me, "*Wanna change places*?"

In an instant, turning fifty was no longer a problem. Sadie was my teacher. I got it.

Ten years later, turning sixty *was* a problem for me. Sadie wasn't around to coach me.

Chapter Twenty

Domestic Partners

In 1993, Mayor Dinkins made domestic partnerships available to same sex couples in New York City. As soon as it was announced, Beryl, who I'd been living with for nine years, and I ran down to the Brooklyn Municipal Building to register. It gave us hospital visitation rights, tenancy privileges, and health benefits. As meager as these stipulations were, we wanted them. We saw it as a first step toward formalizing our relationship.

It was August 26th, 1993 when we appeared at the Marriage Bureau. There was a huge crowd. We were ushered way around the corner to a solitary office where we were the only ones present. We provided proof that we were eligible for a domestic partnership, we signed the forms, and in so doing became domestic partners. The certificate would come in the mail. With no ceremony, it was accomplished.

I was working as a Guidance Counselor/Psychologist at Columbus High School near Pelham Parkway in a middle-class neighborhood in the Bronx. Famous graduates were Anne Bancroft, Sal Mineo, John McGiver, and the first transsexual, Christine Jorgensen.

My principal published a weekly school newsletter that was distributed to the staff at large. He asked for snippets of personal information that he would include. I sent this to his office:

Robert F. Scherma of the Guidance Department and Beryl Schonberger have formalized their relationship and became Domestic Partners pursuant to the laws of New York City.

I thought I was being evasive. Beryl is a name that could be male or female. I wasn't fully out to the faculty-at-large or to students. It was a struggle. I wanted to be out to staff and kids, but I was afraid. Fear paralyzed me. I had one foot in the water and one out. It was time to jump in.

This is what my principal printed in the next newsletter:

Dr. Robert F. Scherma of the Guidance Department and Mr. Beryl Schonberger have formalized their relationship and became domestic partners pursuant to the laws of New York City. Congratulations!

Now, I was out to the entire faculty. My friends offered me good wishes and the guidance department had a celebration, cake and all. But, on occasion, a previously friendly teacher would, all of a sudden, look the other way. It hurt. Prejudice on a personal level always hurts. Sometimes, it enrages.

There was one history teacher who talked about my sexuality in a derisive way in front of his class. One of my students was in that class and reported back to me. Furious, I ran up to his classroom and called him out to the hall and demanded to know why he was discussing my sexuality with his students. He denied it. I told him that my students tell me *everything* and that I didn't believe him.

Coming out is process of small-steps-taken, especially for a child of the 1950s like me. I envy young people today who simply are who they are and let the chips fall where they may. I know the world can still be a nasty and violent place and that tolerance is not universal, but it's better than it was. I saw my own internalized homophobia as I half-heartedly came out to the staff via my principal's newsletter. He celebrated my gayness in a way I was unable to publicly. Maybe I knew he would on some unconscious level. Yet I was fearful and loathed the part of me that was still hesitant. Slowly but surely, I was out to my students, parents, and staff. It was just another fact about me; Dr. Scherma is gay and he has a lover, Beryl. This picture was up in my office and one of my favorite students, Helen, remarked, "Doc, Beryl's handsome!"

I flashed a smile at her.

One afternoon, outside my office some teens were horsing around while I was doing some paperwork. Two kids called each other "faggot." I looked up from my desk and bellowed from my office, "We do not use words like 'nigger,' 'spic,' 'retard,' or 'faggot' in this office!"

José said, "Sorry, Doc, you're right."

Erika reiterated, "Sorry, Doc."

I paused. A grin ran across my face. I gazed at Beryl's picture. Then I looked down and returned to the paperwork at hand.

It was clear who was the brains of the outfit. Beryl had an I.Q. of 150 and a photographic memory. Now, I was no slouch with my 137 I.Q., but being a psychologist who has administered I.Q. exams, I knew those thirteen points made a huge difference. He knew everything, I mean, everything. Whatever passed in front of his eyes, he could recall. I, on the other hand, had a mind like a sieve. When I taught Greek mythology in Latin class, I would have to memorize the names of every goddamned god and goddess each and every time before teaching them. I could memorize thousands of forms for every noun, adjective, and verb, but what was the Greek name for Diana, goddess of the hunt or the Roman name of Athena, goddess of wisdom? When I was younger, I wanted to sing and play guitar for a living, only I couldn't memorize certain lyrics. I sang *Mr. Bojangles* a thousand times and always had to have the sheet music in front of me. But Beryl was the complete opposite. If anyone needed a piece of information, they'd bypass me and go straight to him.

Someone would ask, "What's the capital of Maine?"

He would instantaneously reply, "Augusta."

"And West Virginia?"

"Charleston."

I would have to pull out that place mat of the U.S.A. with all the capitals on it or run to the Almanac I bought Beryl each year. This was before Google.

If someone asked, "How do you convert Fahrenheit to centigrade?"

He'd say matter-of-factly, "That's simple. Centigrade equals Fahrenheit minus 32 times five over nine. Let's say it's 86 degrees Fahrenheit. So, centigrade equals 86 minus 32, times five over nine, then centigrade equals 54 times five over nine, so centigrade equals 30 degrees."

I would have to research the conversion formulas we learned back in high school; he could simply recall them. I would ask him, "Is there anything you don't know?"

Even the children of our friends would call him to ask some arcane fact.

"Beryl, I have a homework assignment. I need a definition of a *palindrome* and a few examples. Can you help me?" Eric, gifted at age 10, would ask.

"Sure. A palindrome is a word or sentence that reads the same forward as it does backwards. Here are some examples:

radar
racecar
Hannah
lepers repel
senile felines
step on no pets
Madam in Eden, I'm Adam
A man, a plan, a canal: Panama"

I knew what a palindrome was but could only recall "radar" or "refer." I thought, *Where the hell is my book on palindromes?*

We were polar opposites in basic ways. He was an intellectual, thought things out logically, and believed reality was what was in front of him; as mentioned before, he didn't believe in God and an afterlife. He was willing to change unwanted behaviors but didn't care much for underlying causes. I, on the other hand, saw the world primarily through my feelings and intuition. I could be impulsive and then suffer the consequences or reap the benefits. I believed in God and had chosen myself as a seeker. The afterlife? *Of course.* I was introspective and unafraid of facing the truth about myself. These differences made for clashes and eye rolling, yet the relationship worked. What one lacked, the other supplied.

This polarity could be a problem but it also was the glue that kept us together. We respected each other's differences, even though we quarreled about them. We could also laugh at how dissimilar we were. Deep down we liked each other and because of that, we were able to transcend our disparities. We knew we were in the game together, on the same team. We had each other's back.

The contrasts added spice to our sexuality. Sometimes, it was hot, sometimes not so hot, but we loved sex. All of it. In any form. I remember a commercial for Chex cereals. There was an arena, like at a basketball game. A roving reporter, microphone in hand, would interview people in the stands. One person would get up and extol Real Cinnamon Corn Chex, another Cocoa Chex or Vanilla Chex, and still another Honey Nut Chex. There was wild cheering for each. One final woman would get up and declare, "It's all good!" Now there was pandemonium. I told Beryl, "That's us and sex. It's *all* good."

He winked at me. In our monogamy, the fire lasted.

190

Finally, in a relationship, it seems to me that there can be only one star. It was usually me. However, I needed a co-star who was willing to accept second billing. I essentially enjoy people and people generally enjoy me. I was always up for fun. Beryl, though appealing and affable, could, on the other hand, be highly critical of people and certainly didn't suffer fools. If a waiter were incompetent, Beryl's wrath would be upon him. If someone wasn't on time, it was the death sentence. Being "the smart one" was the arena he shined in, and brilliantly so. I gave that to him; I had no choice. While I loved having a font of knowledge and an encyclopedic mind next to me, I can't lie, I also resented it.

Chapter Twenty-One
Loss Comes in so Many Packages

On this summer morning, July 11th, Beryl and I were meeting Ken and his wife, Kathy, for breakfast at the Cottonwood Café on Bleecker Street. I was looking forward to their luscious omelets, their round breakfast sausages, and a side of grits with melted butter and ground black pepper. The bread was always freshly baked and warm. We hadn't been there in a while and we were looking forward to meeting with old friends over a grand breakfast. It was always fun to be together.

I was shaving in the bathroom when the phone rang. Beryl answered it. It was my nephew's wife, Matilda, who lived across the street from my mother in Gravesend. Beryl came over to me.

"Bob, your mom fell."

"*Oh no.* How is she?"

This was becoming a frequent occurrence.

"She may have to go to the hospital. We have to get there. I'll call Ken and cancel breakfast."

Sadie lived alone in a ten-room house and had become accident-prone. She lived on the ground floor of the two-family house and never used the stairs. She used a walker and shuffled along as she passed from room to room. New York was in the middle of a heat wave with ten days of 95-100-degree weather. Sadie had the air conditioners removed because she always felt cold, a common complaint of the elderly.

"Oh, Beryl, I just hate this. She's falling too often. I *fucking* hate hospitals."

"I know, Bob. Let's go."

We got in the 1993 Acadia green Honda Accord and headed to Van Sicklen Street in Brooklyn, the house I grew up in.

It took about 20 minutes to get to there. The house was the fourth on the left. I saw a police car with lights flashing out front. My stomach turned.

I parked the car and entered the opened front door, Beryl behind me. In the foyer, a really good-looking cop met me.

He said gently, "I'm sorry for your loss."

Dumbfounded, "*What?*"

"I'm sorry about your mom."

Getting it, I asked, "Where is she?"

"In the bedroom."

"Thank you."

I entered the bedroom and there was Sadie on the far side of the bed. It looked like she had been in distress and struggled to get relief. She was nude. I asked myself why hadn't someone covered her? I took the top sheet and covered her.

I turned to Beryl, "You didn't tell me…"

"I knew you'd be driving and didn't want you to be upset and distracted."

"Matilda told me that Aunt Jo called as she did every Sunday morning. There was only a busy signal. She called Matilda and Doug across the street. They came over and found her dead. She called us to tell you."

It slowly sunk in. A towering, loving force in my life left me. I had turned 50 the previous April and Sadie witnessed all the vicissitudes of my life. Now I would have to face life without her, without my Sadie.

I was incredulous.

I was an orphan now. I felt that I had gone up a notch on the food chain and was no longer protected. I had lived under the illusion that when a parent is alive, your inevitable demise is far away. Now that safeguard was gone. I experienced a new vulnerability I hadn't known up until then.

Another feeling arose, one of expansiveness, as if now the sky above was vast and far-reaching. It was a strange reaction to me. A concomitant feeling was relief. My mother insisted on living alone in a big house in the years after my dad died. I now realized how stressful that situation was to me. I saw that I was always afraid that someone would break into the house and do God knows what. I was fearful that she would fall and no one would know, that she wouldn't be able to press her Medic Alert button. I was afraid that she would need immediate medical attention but wouldn't be able to tell anyone. Now that worry was gone.

The Thursday before, I made a visit to see Sadie. I was in the mood to do some chores for her. She knew when I was in this mood she should not question it and simply thank her lucky stars. She asked me to vacuum and dust the living room and the front porch. She asked me to take down some wall decorations and wash them. She asked me to take out the garbage. After a few hours, I felt it was enough and Sadie said, "Just one more thing…"

I answered, "No, Sadie, it's enough. Let's have some coffee."

She knew not to push further, "Okay, Robert."

Out came the coffee. We chatted and simply enjoyed each other's company. It was a sweet morning. And now it was time to leave.

"Okay, Sadie, I gotta go. Enjoy the rest of the day. I love you."

"Thank you, Robert, for everything. I appreciate it. I love you, too."

She lifted her cheek to be kissed, which I did dutifully. I smiled and said, "See ya, Mom."

When I first arrived that Thursday morning, I had gone to a French bakery on Avenue U near Ocean Parkway. I got Sadie her favorites; two lemon meringue tarts and two Charlotte Russes. On Sunday, after my brothers came and we started to make arrangements for the funeral, I went to the refrigerator and opened the door. There was a half of a lemon meringue tart and half of a Charlotte Russe. Apparently, Sadie was saving these last leftovers for later. I said, "Sadie, I'll eat these two in your honor!" and I did.

It took a year to sell the house; I was in charge of the sale. I would come from time to time and sit in the kitchen and do some paperwork. The quiet and aloneness allowed me to fall into a reverie about moments gone by. Sadie and Frank were now dead. I had to live with that new actuality.

My heart was filled with tears and laughter. *Tears* that they were both gone, never to be seen again. *Laughter* that I got to have so much fun with them all those years.

*

Gloria and Ted

It was Beryl's two-week vacation and our first summer in our new home in Springs, a sleepy hamlet in East Hampton. We lived a mile away from where Jackson Pollock had painted and where many other abstract expressionists worked their craft in what was considered unsurpassed sunlight.

Early afternoon, Beryl and I went to the East Hampton Cinema and picked up tickets for the first showing of *Saving Private Ryan*, which was opening the next day. It was time for lunch, so we crossed over to Newtown Lane and picked up some goodies at the Barefoot Contessa and headed home.

"Let's eat and then go to the beach," Beryl said. I thought that sounded "just dandy," as Beryl was wont to say.

We went home, got out some Sauvignon Blanc and put out the grilled shrimp with lime and cilantro, the snap pea and green bean salad, and some sourdough bread. We put out some extra virgin olive oil for ample bread dipping. Halfway through lunch, the telephone rang. I answered it. It was my brother, Ron, age sixty; he had rented a house in Sag Harbor with his wife and son. He was twenty minutes away.

I was apprehensive because my oldest brother, Ted, age sixty-eight, was on life support at Newark Medical Center. He had been in the hospital, waiting for a heart transplant since March. We discovered the ghoulish practice of waiting for a holiday weekend when most accidents occurred. Easter and Memorial Day and 4th of July weekends were harvesting times. Ted had a successful heart transplant on July 5th. The young man died in a motorcycle accident, he was barely out of his teens. The parents signed over his heart, so my brother could live. However, Ted contracted M.R.S.A., a strain of staph bacteria resistant to antibiotics. This is a common occurrence in hospitals where invasive surgeries take place after an extended stay. For one month, the medical staff sent in infectious disease specialists all to no avail. There was nothing more to be done.

"Hello."

"It's Ron. It's time. They're going to pull the plug tonight when Frank comes in from L.A. We should go soon."

Ron was the brother closest in age to me. I was five years younger. It was the end of the road for Ted, our oldest brother.

It was the call we hoped would never be made and here it was. Ted had three sons and a daughter and his wife, Gloria, who was with him every step of the way. Each of them was told to meet at the hospital. Frank was the oldest son who was flying in from Los Angeles and when he arrived, we would pull the plug.

"I'll pick you up, Ron. It's on the way. Did you call Mickey?"

Mickey, age 66, was the second oldest brother; he lived on Staten Island.

"I didn't."

"I'll call him and then leave to pick you up."

I put the phone down, "Beryl, they're pulling the plug tonight. I'm going. Do you want to go?"

I knew the answer already.

"No, I'll stay behind and wait for you to return."

I knew Beryl would be in tears the whole time, which I had seen when he was at my dad's funeral in 1990 and when his father faded away in a nursing home and when his mother recovered in a trauma unit for three weeks after a car accident not knowing if she would make it. He felt things too deeply.

"Okay. I need to call Mickey."

I looked up his number and called him, "Mick, this is it. They're pulling the plug. Ron and I are going to the hospital. Do you want to come?"

"No, I just can't witness another death."

Not only had our dad and mom died in 1990 and 1993, but in 1991, his wife, Delia, died at age fifty-eight. He was bereft since then.

"Call me when it's done."

"Okay, Mick. Will do."

I got my wallet, a bottle of Poland Spring water, my Motorola flip phone, and my keys. I kissed Beryl goodbye. He walked me to the front door.

"Drive safely, hon. I love you."

"I love you, too, Beryl."

I got into the car, drove to the street, turned around, and waved goodbye. Beryl waved back. I made a right and then another right and headed to Route 114 to pick up my brother, Ron.

"Ron, I have to stop and get gas before we get on the highway."

"Okay."

I filled the tank and we were off to Newark Medical Center. It was a three-hour drive and it was now late afternoon.

"This is going to be hard."

"I know, Rob."

"This is the first brother to go... I don't like it."

"It's awful." And then, "It's good we'll be there as he leaves."

"The only thing keeping him alive is a machine. He's brain-dead. He already left. It's so sad, Ron."

For most of the trip, we were in silence. I drove as if in a trance mulling over M.R.S.A., previous heart attacks, the trips to so many hospitals, the installations of his pacemaker and defibrillator, and ultimately, the heart transplant... a rough journey which lead to this moment where it felt it was all for naught. In the car, there was little to say and no words for what we were about to do. We reached the hospital early evening. Gloria was there and so were Doug and Tom and Krystyne...three of their children. The only one missing was Frank who was on a flight to Newark International Airport from L.A.

We met in Ted's room where a ventilator was moving air into and out of his lungs. The pneumatic compressions delivered room-air several times a minute. The sounds of mechanical breathing reminded us of the task at hand, a reminder we didn't want or need. I felt paralyzed for a short time but was drawn away from the moment as we started hugging each other and saying barely anything.

197

"Let's go down for a cup of coffee," Gloria proffered. "Frank won't be here for several hours."

"Good idea," Ron said.

We went downstairs by elevator and had some coffee and a piece of cherry pie; some had a sandwich or a salad.

"This is going to be a long night," Tom said.

"It sure is," Doug responded.

We reminisced about how we used to kid Ted about the heart he would eventually get. If he started to rap and say, "Yo, yo, yo, what the dillio," he obviously got a *black* heart. Or if he started to meditate and chant Ommmmmmm, clearly it must be an *Asian* heart. Or if he had a compulsion to dance salsa, evidently an *Hispanic* heart. And if he suddenly had an urge to interior decorate, yep, a *gay* heart.

We laughed and it broke the tension. After a while, we went back upstairs to Ted's room. The up and down measured motion of the ventilator and the accompanying sounds greeted us. We sat about the room and soon Frank walked in.

"Hi, everybody!"

He was dressed in khakis and a white shirt, was tanned, but looked pallid and ashen. He was here, and now the moment had arrived.

The cardiologist who cared for Ted these past six months was present and said, "Please gather round Ted." We stood flanked out to the right and left of him as Dr. Joseph disengaged the ventilator. The eerie noise of the machinery slowed down and eventually came to a complete stop a half hour later. At that moment, Ted was pronounced dead.

Sons and daughter hugged mother, nephews and niece hugged uncles, brothers and sister hugged each other, and Ted's two brothers and Gloria hugged one another.

After several moments, when the deed was done and we had somehow reassembled as the family left behind, we took comfort in being together.

I separated from the family and stood by Ted's body. I held his hand. I thought, *My oldest brother is gone. Ted is gone.* I felt the loss immediately and profoundly. Tears welled up. I couldn't let go of his hand.

"I don't believe this. How can there only be three of us when we were always four?

Loss comes in so many packages. My dad, gone. My mom, gone. And now, Ted. I remember when I was a young teen, I razzed my three older brothers in sing-song fashion, "You're all gonna die first and I'm goin' to die last! You poor guys." I didn't know what I knew now. A brother dies, and I'm left behind with loneliness, hurt, and fear. I was desolate and forsaken. There was nothing anyone could say or do to ease the pain.

Ron and I decided to drive back to the Hamptons. I dropped him off and got home at three a.m. Beryl was asleep. I just wanted to be near him. He had a brother who died, he understood. I woke up at nine o'clock the next morning and Beryl came back to bed and said, "Bob, I'll do whatever you want to do today."

I thought for a moment and said, "I want to go to the movies. I want to see *Saving Private Ryan*."

I needed to step back into my life for a moment, especially since the memorial service was going to be in a few days. To me, a movie theater is like a temple, or a church, where one can feel safe in anonymity. Cinema reveals truths or humor or life's struggles. I needed to be in the dark.

Beryl said, "Sure, Bob. We'll do that."

He put his arm around me and kissed my forehead. We went downstairs to breakfast.

By noon, we were in the theater. *Saving Private Ryan* was a World War II movie. Following the Normandy Landings, a group of U.S. soldiers go behind enemy lines to retrieve a paratrooper whose brothers have been killed in action. I only lost one brother but wondered about my other two. What would it be like to lose all my brothers? I shuddered at the thought.

I reached out for Beryl's hand.

I love you.
I love you, too, Bob.

Beryl on Couch

Beryl had a penchant for being prone. He loved to sneak in a nap whenever he could, especially at the house in East Hampton. Being handy, he also loved watching the House and Garden network or any home improvement show in this horizontal position. On Saturday mornings, Beryl would get up early, make tea and cinnamon toast, and luxuriate in reading the yesterday's newspapers or the latest edition of East Hampton's *Dan's Papers,* a local weekly. I would shower and shave upstairs, get dressed, and head downstairs and ready myself to do some morning shopping, including buying the *Times* and the *New York Post.* I'd put on my jacket, gather my keys and shoulder bag, and prepare to leave.

Beryl was shy by nature, contrary to what people thought who saw him as outgoing and sociable. He could be uneasy when meeting new people. He retreated from public displays of affection, even in the privacy of his own home. He was slow to be touched affectionately, as if not feeling worthy of being cared about. Coming from the kitchen counter, I'd forewarn him.

"Beryl, I'm coming over to the sofa and I'm going to hold your hand."

He'd tense up and before he knew it, I'd reached over the sofa and hold his hand. Gazing at him with a smile, I'd extend an adoring glance. Each time I did this, the same thing would happen. He'd look up at me, smile broadly, and turn beet red. I'd pause for a long moment and then I'd say, "Honey, I'm going out for the papers and a few other things."

Still a shade of crimson, he would grin.

Then he'd say, "Okay, honey. And if you see a jelly doughnut, please buy me one."

Smiling, "Of course, my love."

I'd finally let go of his hand and his face would return to its normal color. He would then get up to take me to the door.

Each time I would say, "You don't have to get up, Beryl..."

He'd say, "Oh, no, I must."

And then, "Drive safely."

Like clockwork.

"Okay, honey, I'll be back in a little while. I love you."

"I love you, too, Bob."

I'd get into the car, turn the engine on, drive to the street, stop for a moment, and turn around to wave goodbye. Beryl would always be there to wave back as he did this morning. He then would return to the sofa and in his supine position, he would watch another episode of *This Old House* on P.B.S. as he eagerly awaited the arrival of his jelly doughnut.

Once I asked Beryl why he insisted on taking me to the door each and every time I left the house alone. He paused and then said,

"It might be the last time I see you."

Commemorating the day we met in 1984, Beryl and I always celebrated our anniversary on December 13th at a fine restaurant. Our favorite was *One if by Land, Two if by Sea.* It's Aaron Burr's landmark carriage house located on Barrow Street in the Village. It's a romantic spot, the service is impeccable, and the food a total delight. It was 2004, our twentieth anniversary and we invited our close friends, Beryl [yes, another Beryl] and Gail, our treat. We loved each other as only good friends could.

One if by Land has a prix fixe menu. First, there are the appetizers. Among them you could have grilled octopus, seared *foie gras*, a mission fig salad, or oxtail tortellini. Or the smoked Spanish mackerel, which I had. It was spaghetti squash and pickled cherries in a rhubarb puree. Then you had to choose an *entrée*. Their house special was Beef Wellington. You could also select steamed black sea bass, roasted breast of duck, yellowtail snapper, slow-cooked pork loin, a risotto, and oven-roasted chicken breast or rack of lamb as well. My lover, Beryl, had the rack of lamb, his favorite, and I chose the Beef Wellington. The ladies went for seafood.

Beef Wellington is what I mostly ordered over the years there. I rarely ate beef and this was a treat. A centerpiece of filet mignon, which has been laid in a marinade of mushrooms, shallots, garlic, butter, and olive oil, is placed in a hot skillet for a few minutes. A piece of prosciutto is placed on top of that. Then there's the puff pastry. The beef is placed in that and a smattering of *foie gras* is generously smoothed over the beef and then baked. When it arrives at the table it is greeted with *ooohs* and *aaahs* and it is served with fingerling potatoes [yummy] and warm wilted winter greens [healthy].

The meal was nicely paced. The champagne flowed. The appetizers were presented. The *entrées* were served. And then, because everyone was on a diet, except my Beryl, we ordered a cinnamon caramelized apple with pastries and raspberry coulis. The waiter was informed that it was our anniversary, so in chocolate syrup across the top of the serving plate it read, "Happy 20th Anniversary." And it was *happy*.

We sipped our cappuccinos, smiled and laughed the evening away with stories of past travels together and other good times. We were together tonight, and it was good.

*

It was October 10th, 2005, a Monday morning in Brooklyn Heights and I was going to drive Beryl to work. We had been together almost twenty-one years. I loved that he was handsome, slim, articulate, and a gentleman, definitely the class part of the relationship. That was in contrast to me, a swarthy Italian from Gravesend, mischievous, always on a diet, forever in graduate school, and the mystic of the two.

Beryl glanced down at his Cartier watch; he was wearing the less expensive one. It was 9:15 a.m.

He was almost ready to leave when he coughed. He had a viral infection this past week, *but* his cough was way too loud and it scared me. With a look of fright, I asked,

"*Beryl*, what was *that*?"

"I don't know. But I've got to sit down."

Clutching his chest, he sat on the edge of the bed.

"Is there something wrong with your heart?"

This was a question that made no sense. He had routine medical checkups, had blood pressure readings of 110/70 regularly, and his cholesterol levels were under 140.

"No, I have no pain in my arms. I just have to lie down."

"Shall I call your boss and tell him you're not coming in?"

"Yes, call him."

"Do you want a doctor?"

"No, I just want to lie down."

It was now 10:30 a.m. and I had a dermatologist's appointment in the city at noon. I ran it past Beryl.

"Honey, I have an appointment with Carolyn Shear, I can cancel it. Do you want me to stay?"

"No, go."

I went, had a body scan, and got home by one p.m.

"Beryl, do you need anything? Some lunch, some soup?"

"No, I've been throwing up all morning."

I was supposed to meet my friend, Liz, for dinner at four p.m. but I called her and cancelled.

"Do you want to go to the doctor? Maybe Goldstein can tell us what's going on."

"No. Not yet."

Beryl, who was usually robust, cheerful, filled with wit, information, and sarcasm, was ashen, curled in a ball, morose, almost lifeless. The only time he moved was to lurch up and run to the bathroom to vomit.

It was now about three p.m. and he was lying still on the bed. The lights were out. His head peeked out from under the paisley comforter. He was awake, barely.

"Do you want me to go downstairs and get you some wanton soup?"

"Maybe later. I just need to sleep."

The bedroom was dark, black. I looked out of the window at the New York City skyline searching for...an answer to an overwhelming yet unformed question. Beryl would refer to the city's skyscraper as Oz as we returned from his family in Allentown. But tonight, Oz did not glitter.

The autumnal evening was descending and its purples and grays seemed uninviting, almost cold, ominous. Something was not right and I dared not ask what it was.

After a few minutes, I told Beryl that I was going downstairs to see a movie across the street. The Brooklyn Heights Cinema was playing *Proof.* A film, a darkened theater, some malt balls always soothed me. I told Beryl I'd bring up wanton soup afterwards. I knew when Beryl was sick, he didn't want to be doted on, hovered over. I was a natural hoverer. I resisted and went down to see Gwyneth Paltrow and Anthony Hopkins.

After this somber movie, I went to Fortune House up the block and picked up the Wanton Soup and a Schweppes Ginger Ale. I returned to the apartment and went into the bedroom. No lights were on. Beryl was still in bed but awake.

I asked, "How are you feeling?"

"Nauseous."

I told him I had some soup and ginger ale. He sipped some ginger ale through a straw and couldn't hold it down. He ran to the toilet and threw up again.

"Honey, just lie down. I'll be inside. I'll drop by every so often."

I put the soup in the refrigerator in the hope that he would be able to ingest something, *anything,* later on. I sat on the auburn leather couch on call.

I watched C.N.N. I read the Post and the Times. After *Seinfeld*, I went to bed. Beryl opened his eyes when I slipped under the covers.

"You okay, honey? Need anything?"

"No, I'll just sleep."

We both slept on and off that night and when we got up Tuesday morning, Beryl spoke out.

"I think we should go see Goldstein."

"Good."

We dressed, went down to the car in the basement garage, and drove into the city to see our doctor. Thank, God.

Goldstein's office was on Fifth Avenue at 14th Street. He was my doctor when I lived in the city and became Beryl's as well shortly after we met in 1984.

I couldn't readily park, so I dropped off Beryl in front of the office and parked the car in a garage. By the time I arrived in the office, Beryl had already had an E.K.G. Goldstein said that it looked like a heart attack, but the fact that he had this ongoing viral infection could mean it was something else. He took a second E.K.G. This time he was concerned. He said we ought to go to St. Vincent's E.R. around the corner. Just to be sure. Have an echocardiogram and let's see what their cardiologists had to say. He spoke calmly and without alarm. He said he'd call ahead and left the examining room.

Beryl and I stood facing each other. He looked at me, searching almost pleading. He looked afraid. I was petrified and hoped I didn't show it. He looked down and pondered aloud, "I don't want to be a heart patient. I don't want to live like that."

Fear turned to sadness and resignation. Had he given up? A picture came flashing across my mind; my friend, Paul, said those very words, "I don't want to live like that," after he found out he had to quit his job, live in a wheelchair in his sister's home for the rest of his life. Diabetes and kidney failure had done him in and this was the final blow. He checked out of the planet a few days later. He was only thirty-nine, that was 1982. This wasn't going to happen again, was it? I held back.

"No, Beryl. Let's just go to the E.R. and let them do what they have to do and we'll *handle* this."

He needed an anchor and that was me. I simply went into action mode and felt nothing. I couldn't or I'd fall apart.

We left the office, got on the elevator from the sixteenth floor, and seemingly stopped at every other floor. People entered and the car became crowded. Beryl and I kept silent. Just get to the hospital. An eternity passed by the time we finally reached the ground floor. I hailed a cab and in two minutes we were in St. Vincent's E.R. A security guard gave us forms and we filled them out and waited our turn. I got Beryl a small bottle of water from the vending machine and again, we waited.

Several minutes passed by and I was becoming impatient. I said to Beryl, "Why aren't they calling you? Should I go over and ask?"

Beryl said, "Don't get crazy. Stay calm."

He knew I could have a short fuse when under pressure, especially in the face of an unfeeling bureaucracy.

"If this is a triage area, why aren't they calling you? You had heart pains."

Beryl was too tired to fight me.

I said, "Let me see if I can speed things up a little."

I went to the admitting nurse, who was behind the Plexiglas. I stood there in plain sight. She ignored me. She was working at the computer facing me and called in another patient. I went back to where Beryl was sitting. I was ready to kick in the window, call her a motherfucking bitch, and demand immediate medical attention. However, I went to the window again and tapped on it. I got her attention. I handed her a note, which said that Beryl could be in the middle of a heart attack. I was fuming but couldn't show it. I thought, *Hadn't she read this on the initial forms we handed in? God damn it!*

When she read the note, her eyes widened and she called him in at once.

She was polite and solicitous as can be. I just clenched my jaw.

208

His paperwork was processed and he was sent into the I.C.U. I had to wait outside until he was in a bed and seen by the cardiologist and attending physicians. I asked a second officious security guard if he'd call me when I could go in and see Beryl. He asked, "Who are you?" I said I was his domestic partner. He stiffened a bit and said almost indifferently, "Okay." After forty-five minutes, I got up to look for the guard and was told he left for the day. So much for the kindness of strangers.

In the I.C.U., Beryl was hooked up to an I.V. They took an echocardiogram, a test that uses sound waves to create a moving picture of the heart so that assessment of heart functioning could be readily determined. I was told that he had significant serum elevations, cardiomegaly, hemopericardium, and a large transmural acute myocardial infarction. What were they talking about? All I knew was that he was in deep shit.

Since his heart was constricting, he was in great pain. So, they administered a large dosage of morphine. Within ten seconds, Beryl was in major distress. The medical staff swirled around him, worked furiously, and finally brought him to a state of calm. No one explained what just occurred. I was just happy he was lying there stoned out of his mind with a broad grin on his face. I'm sorry I didn't have his Jimi Hendrix L.Ps. I could imagine him fake playing the electric guitar with head and shoulders swaying in synch with the beat and his lips pursed and his head bobbing. After all this time, he still turned me on. I had a thing for skinny guys, he, for beefy.

Goldstein had my cell number, so he called me up. He said that he would move Beryl into St. Vincent's Cardiac Care Unit. He had had a heart attack and this would be the best option. Cardiologists would monitor his condition 24/7. They were waiting for a bed and that would take a few hours.

Our friends at the time, Tina and Rick from Scranton, were supposed to visit us at our house in East Hampton. I called Tina to tell her we had to cancel. I told her Beryl was in the hospital, had had a heart attack, would be moved to C.C.U., and that everything was under control.

"He's right here, I'm not supposed to have the phone on. I'll let you speak with him for a minute."

Tina and Beryl were longtime friends from Beryl's days at Temple University. They were stoned together for most of the late sixties. They had upper crust personas that they often used for fun.

"*Charles*, is that you?"

"*Catherine*, is that you?"

"How *are* you?"

"I'm really high."

"Shouldn't we all be? I *love* you."

"I love you, too. Give my regards to L'il Rickie."

"And you, give mine to Broadway."

It was now 7:30 p.m. I got into a conversation with a German woman with short-cropped blond hair, an athletic appearance and a crisp manner. She was there for a friend. She'd been visiting a New York City friend when her friend had a stroke. I explained that Beryl had a heart attack.

"I'm leaving for Berlin tomorrow but I want to make sure my friend is cared for. I've notified her sister who'll be here tomorrow."

We parted and now it was 9:30 p.m. Both her friend and Beryl were still in the I.C.U. I was getting edgy. I wanted to go home. I wanted to get out of there. I was going to tell Beryl I'd see him tomorrow when I bumped into my German friend again.

"I'm going to go home. I can't stand the waiting anymore. I'll come back tomorrow," I told her.

"No!" she bellowed, "I'm going to stay till my friend is in her room."

That, "No!" shook me. It was as if a *voice* was giving me a directive, *stay*. And so, I stayed.

By 11:30 p.m., Beryl was in the C.C.U. fully set up. They told me I could see him. We chatted. He said he was comfortable. I said I'd come tomorrow. He said don't come until early afternoon because they'd most likely be working on him. So, I said I'd be there about one p.m. and spend the day. I had some chores to do and a few phone calls to make. No one but Tina and Rick knew Beryl was in the hospital.

I kissed Beryl on the forehead and said, "I love you, honey. I'll see you tomorrow."

"I love you, Bob."

I walked out of the hospital a little after midnight, Wednesday morning, October 12th. Somewhere between leaving the hospital and the car ride home to Brooklyn, a terrifying thought came into my mind, *Beryl's going to die*. I told myself to get this thought out of my head. That couldn't happen, it *wouldn't* happen. My father was dead. My mother was dead. My brother, Ted, was dead. My brother, Mick, just died in July. Dear God, not again. Not *Beryl*.

After I parked the car, I got home and lay down on my side of the bed and remembered that *God gives to His beloved in sleep*. It's a great act of faith. I closed my eyes and slept.

The next morning, the phone ringing roused me. I was dreaming, but what of? I stood up and scooted over to the phone, which was on Beryl's side of the bed. I wanted to get it before the answering machine picked up. I got it in time. I looked over to the clock radio. It was 7:30 a.m.

"Hello," I said.

"Hi, Bob?"

"Yes, it's me."

"It's Paul Goldstein. I'm at the hospital. I have some bad news to tell you, quite shocking news actually."

"What, Paul?" I asked.

"Beryl died ten minutes ago."

*

I sat down on the edge of the bed. My jaw dropped. I stopped breathing. I became aware that tears were falling down my face. I couldn't, *didn't* hear anything he said after that. My life, with those words, was irrevocably changed. My Berly-boy was gone. In that moment, I recalled Sadie murmuring after my dad Frank died, "You weren't supposed to die without me. You promised."

Her heart was broken. And now, so was mine.

"Bob, I think you ought to come down to the hospital. He's in C.C.U. where you were last night. Come now. I'll be waiting for you."

I said, "Okay," and hung up. *Click.*

A long, stunned silence. I couldn't breathe. I stood up. To go where?

I had to steady myself on the end table. I had to hold on. Hold on to what?

I thought, *I have to tell people.* I made phone calls and then others made phone calls. The word was out. Beryl was dead. Some close friends and family met me at St. Vincent's. They were there when I arrived. Paul Goldstein greeted us. He explained that Beryl had an uneventful night. He slept well. At seven a.m., he woke up in distress. He pushed the alert button. The medical staff came running. He was in cardiac arrest. They tried their best. They couldn't save him. He was pronounced dead at 7:20 a.m.

One of the attending cardiologists entered the room. I asked him if he could get his wedding band off his finger. He worked and worked and finally got it off. He gave it to me. I smiled and said thank you.

I decided to call Riverside Memorial Chapel. A woman staff member said only family members could make funeral arrangements, especially regarding cremation. I told them we were domestic partners in New York City. She said, "However, you're not married. Family has to make these decisions." I said I *was* his family. Besides, I told her, his mother had dementia. I got off the phone.

My friend, Gail, got on the phone and prevailed upon them. She told them that a domestic partnership was a lawful agreement and is fully recognized in New York City. Gail's authoritative insistence and clarity convinced them. She was the external voice I couldn't access within myself. The problem was I had decided on cremation and their legal concern was if a family member objected, they'd be liable. Gail said Beryl's mother was in a home with dementia and his family gave full assent to my funeral arrangements. In addition, we had been together twenty-one years. They gave in. When I got on the phone, they asked that I bring proof of domestic partnership the next day.

On Friday night before the funeral, I went to the chapel with my sister-in-law, Gloria. She has a heart as big as all Texas and her presence comforted me. We got there a little early and since it was the Jewish *Sabbath*, the place was empty. An undertaker greeted us and took us to the basement floor. He ushered us into a room where Beryl's body was. There was Beryl in a white shroud, only his head peeked out. He was in a pine box with a dark blanket covering him; it had a huge Star of David emblazoned on it.

There seemed to be a hint of a smile on his face.

I looked at Beryl and turned to Gloria.

"Doesn't he look like he's at peace?"

"Yes, he does," she answered, "it looks like he's smiling."

I was exhilarated and said, "I don't care if this feeling lasts only fifteen minutes, but I feel he's really at rest and at peace. I'm okay with his dying."

Filled with mischief and a penchant for documenting everything, I asked, "Gloria, do you think I could take pictures of his body?"

She said smiling, "Rob, do your thing."

And so, I did. I had my Raz-r flip phone camera and I took four photos. I documented everything all my life and this was just me doing what I always did.

On Saturday morning, I went into silence and gathered my thoughts. I put together my eulogy. I selected some music and created a C.D. for the service. I did a loop, including Samuel Barber's *Adagio for Strings*. I sat at the computer in a trance. I stared at the screen but didn't see it. I was now in another country and I didn't know the language. I was bewildered and overwhelmingly lonely. How would I go on without him?

I took refuge in a thought from *A Course in Miracles*, "Your passage through time and space is not at random. You cannot but be in the right place at the right time."

My Eternal Companion was there with me.

"I am here."
Every step of the way.
It had always been so.
I knew it wouldn't be different now.

In the afternoon, family came over. Someone brought flowers. Someone brought food. My great nephew, Grayson, crawled about the living room floor. The day passed into evening. We went out to eat at Chez Henri downstairs. We went home. It was okay when I was with people, but alone, I had to face my new reality and I didn't want to.

I went out on the terrace and looked out. It seemed like everything was the same, except nothing was.

Soon it was Sunday morning, October 16th. I had some breakfast, showered and shaved, got dressed, and drove to Riverside Memorial Chapel. I parked the car. The first person I saw was Beryl's sister from California. My heart leapt up. We hugged and then walked across the street to the chapel where the five Allentown kids, her grandchildren, were standing each in corners. I asked why this was so and Joshua, the eldest, said, "We're being chastised." I laughed. I hugged them. I went into the chapel and throngs of people greeted me. I spoke to each and every last one of them. It was a love fest. Soon, the lobby was too crowded; there was tension in the room. I didn't expect so many people. The staff changed plans. Three hundred were present; they directed us to the largest chapel upstairs.

Samuel Barber's music filled the chapel as we assembled. I got up, went to the podium, and looked out at those in front of me. I thought love was in the room. These were family and friends. I knew each one of them. I loved them and they loved me. And we came together today because of our love for Beryl. Today, we were one.

I paused a moment, pulled out my notes, and began:

When I was in the seminary as a young man studying for the Roman Catholic priesthood, I had an English professor, a priest who was a wistful soul who asked us to read 'The Little Prince' as literature and books like 'Franny and Zooey.' He would talk about contemporary love songs where there is a proclamation to the world that somebody, out there, loved us, finally. He felt that this jubilation belied the fact that we fundamentally felt unlovable and unworthy of love. He pointed out that our job was to undo that basic mistaken belief and reassert how truly loveable we are in God's eyes. And so, God sends us people to remind us: parents, brothers and sisters, children, relatives, friends, lovers. For me, God sent an abundance of love in many forms in my 62 years. And, he sent me Beryl.

Early in our relationship, Beryl showed me a vulnerability that he tried to hide. I am happy that I got to see that vulnerability and that he felt safe with me. And I know he felt safe with me even to his last day on planet earth.

Beryl and I were not ones for public celebrations, it was not our way. In December 2000, we decided to privately exchange vows. We did it at the house in East Hampton; we lit a fire, sipped some wine, and exchanged rings. Here is what we said. I read my vows first.

Come, grow old with me from time to beyond time.

Let us join in celebrating peace by demanding no sacrifice of each other; for you offer me the love I offer you.

Let us lose the fear of recognizing our love for each other.

Let us be one and not apart.

Let the Holy Spirit enter our relationship and loving be the goal we attain.

Sometimes profound commitments are left unsaid.

Let us speak our love for each other in front of God and man and each other.

And so, with these rings I thee wed.

May our marriage and our love grow.

So, you see, I have a flourish of words; I can't say it simply. but Beryl is straight to the point. Here is what he said:

Bob, I love you and I want to be with you for the rest of my life.

And he was.

Chapter Twenty-Two

Mourning

As I listened to some melancholic music of Leonard Cohen and his soulful lyrics one day, I went back in time and realized that I never said *goodbye* to Beryl.

I was taken aback, despondent, in profound pain.

I didn't know that would be the last weekend we'd spend at our house in the Hamptons.

I didn't know when I ordered Mussels that it would be the last time you'd break up your roll and soak the pieces in my garlic sauce.

I didn't know when you scrubbed my back and I scrubbed yours that it would be the last time we'd shower together.

I didn't know that would be the last time we would visit your niece, Joelle and Gary, and the five kids in Allentown.

I didn't know that was the last fight we would ever have.

I didn't know when we were celebrating my Aunt Josie's 90th birthday with my entire family it would be your last celebration with the Scherma clan.

I didn't know as I pulled out my camera phone at Aunt Josie's party and took a picture of you that it would be the last one I'd ever take of you.

I didn't know that would be the last time we'd shop at Short Hills Mall.

I didn't know that would be the last time we'd look out at the New York City skyline together from our Brooklyn Heights apartment.

I didn't know that would be the last night we'd sleep in the same bed.

I didn't know we'd spend our last day together at the hospital.

I didn't know that was the last time it would be Beryl and Bob or Bob and Beryl.

I didn't know that night would be the last time you would speak with me and I would speak with you.

I didn't know when Paul Goldstein called me Wednesday morning at 7:30 a.m. that he would say you left us.

When Beryl died, my world screeched to a halting stop.

Since I was overwhelmed, I did what I usually do under such circumstances, I go into action. After I notified people, I went to the hospital, made funeral arrangements, talked to the rabbi, put a C.D. together for the service, and spent time with family and friends. I was living on the edge of my existence, almost in a trance, going through the motions as if alive. Who was I now if I wasn't Bob and Beryl? How would I face each morning, each afternoon, each evening, each night without the love of my life? There was too much feeling, but I couldn't feel. I thought I would die if I let the pain come through. Unlike Joan Didion upon hearing the news of her husband's death, I was not *a cool customer*, but I acted like one.

On Thursday, I put a sign up on the bulletin board in the main lobby of my co-op. I wrote that Beryl had died and that funeral services would be held at Riverside Memorial Chapel the following Sunday.

On Friday morning around eight a.m., my doorbell rang. I was still in my bathrobe. I opened the door. It was my neighbor, Dawn, her substantial Jamaican figure in bright multi-colored apparel, her dark brown skin, her dreads, her eyes that sparkle ready for fun, good or bad, and her broad nose all lead you to her luscious, thick lips which cannot contain her teeth that are reminiscent of the ivories on a piano keyboard. I knew her from the hallway and from the mailroom, hello-have-a-good-day kind of friendly. She had her street clothes on and was heading out for work.

"I just found out that Beryl died. I can't believe it. I *just* saw him last week."

She hugged me and held me close, encompassing me as if to protect me.

She then pushed away from me and looked me straight in the eye. With intent and purpose, she paused and then spoke.

"I know where you're going."

I pulled back.

She said it again, "I *know* where you're going."

I didn't quite understand exactly what she meant, but I knew she was to be my teacher. I wasn't sure what she would teach, but I knew she was sent to me, a companion to show me the way. Only, what way? Where was it that I was going? And what did she know that I didn't? I simply believed her with absolute certainty that she was going to teach me something. Something profound.

I was familiar with Jamaican ways at Columbus High School where I had a caseload of students who heralded from Jamaica, documented or not. These teenagers were bright, brazen, readily sucking in their teeth if they didn't like what I said, willing to talk, and always fun. My kind of kids. Their parents could be strict and sometimes unrelentingly tough on their progeny; they expected big things from them. These teenagers came from big families and wanted to make something of themselves so they could take care some of their folks back in Kingston.

When I would encounter Dawn in our building, I found she was warm, engaging, sassy, and feisty, a real live wire who also seemed to have a generous heart. I found out that she was a home nurse and I could tell that her clients were lucky to have her. Yes, they had a force to contend with, she was demanding and they'd better do what they could do or watch out, yet her affection for them was unmistakable. She sometimes visited clients on her own time and was always baking cookies and such for them. Dawn seemed pretty special, yet we remained just neighbors and that seemed to satisfy us.

She knew Beryl.

They liked each other and often met in the laundry room early Sunday mornings before Martha Stewart aired at 8:30 a.m. I would be at the computer in the bedroom after putting up the coffee and Beryl would shout out at 8:28 or so that Martha Stewart's show was imminent, "Mah-thah's going to be on, honey!"

I'd yell out, "I'll be there."

I'd get my coffee [dark, one sweet'n low], Beryl already was sipping his [black, no sugar] and there, we'd sit, absolutely content to listen to Martha describe her *perfect* world, everything *just* right.

The laundry had been done and folded and put away [Beryl always did the laundry because he said he did it better than me. I said, "*Fine.*" I was no fool.] From time to time, he'd mention that he'd seen Dawn in the laundry room. I could imagine them chatting animatedly; two charmers with stories-to-go, whose smiles together could light up both Broadway and all uptown.

Dawn and Beryl and Dawn and I knew each other in this cursory way for about ten years. She knew Beryl better than me.

Days passed. The funeral came on Sunday and Dawn was there. And on Monday and Tuesday nights, I held a *shiva* at the apartment for people who wanted to express their condolences. I loved the Jewish tradition of bringing sweet things to your home to assuage the bitterness of death. Catholics didn't do this, not even fallen away ones. Dawn came both nights and she brought some of her home-baked butter cookies.

One night afterwards, we met at my apartment. We sat down on the leather couch and had some tea; I put out some of the goodies and we chatted about this and that and then I asked her what was on my mind for days.

"Dawn, what did you mean when you told me, 'I know where you are going?'"

She put down her tea and looked at me.

"Well, Bob, I was married to my husband, Bob, yes, *Bob,* too, and he died fifteen years ago unexpectedly and so I know where you are going since I've been there."

I was mesmerized. Beryl's death was so fresh in my experience and I was raw. I was moved by these words. I knew I would not be alone on this journey. Beryl was gone…really gone… How could I fathom this reality? My neighbor would be with me all the way through, of that I was sure. I always felt the people you need appear just when you need them. And Dawn appeared for me.

She visited often, we broke bread, and we talked about what it's like to have the person you love die. She knew. Her Bob was a Swede and they apparently made a striking couple; heads would turn. She missed him very much. They had their fights, it wasn't perfect, but she loved him. Fiercely.

Listening to her story made me feel not so alone. The grieving trip is a long and winding one and you never know when the hurting will break the surface. Dawn was there to be my safety net.

One Sunday night at dusk, we looked out from my terrace at the glimmering New York City skyline. I told her Beryl used to call it *Oz*. The evening sun had settled down and shards of indigo and pumpkin light framed the tip of Manhattan Island. Another awesome moment and I never tired of it.

Dawn looked at me and said, "You know, Bob, Beryl's death gave us something; each other. Before, this friendship didn't exist on this level and now it does. It's almost as if Beryl gave us a gift in his absence."

I smiled at her.

*

The essence of grieving, I have found, is contending with a broken heart.
The Bee Gees asked, *How can you mend a broken heart?*
The Beatles responded, *I get by with a little help from my friends.*

Joshua

Beryl died in October and six weeks later, I was on my way from Brooklyn to Allentown to spend Thanksgiving dinner with his family. We had developed a tradition of spending this holiday in Pennsylvania. And this Thanksgiving, I wanted to see his niece, now my niece, Joelle, and Gary and the five kids. This was the first time I would be going to see Beryl's family without him. I picked up the five large chocolate chip cookies the five kids liked, bought some coffee, got into the car, and drove off, alone.

As I drove to the Holland Tunnel, I asked myself how I would be able to do this. I was used to doing a lot with Beryl for the past twenty-one years, you know, the couple thing. Even when you're not with your partner, your reference point is your partner. He and I did a lot of things independently of each other, especially me; I had to have it that way. Sometimes, I had to be with a friend alone. The conversation changed when both he and I were present. I encouraged him to be with his friends apart from me. His need was not as strong as mine. He always invited me along and I'd say, "Beryl, be with your friends without me. I see them in social situations, now you be with them." He didn't quite get it. And so, independent me said to myself that I could handle this without my Beryl.

As I got onto the New Jersey Turnpike and then onto the long stretch into P.A. on Route 78, I listened to music, I felt sad and abandoned, and soon became ensconced in deep, abiding pain.

After Beryl died, I did most of my grieving on the Long Island Expressway on the way to our house in the Hamptons. Melancholic music led to grieving and then to pain. In both places, Beryl would no longer be. Now, it was just me and I had to continue with my life. And so, I drove to Allentown and was greeted by the oldest kid, Joshua, aged nine and the two sets of twins, one aged five, the younger ones aged two. And kids being kids, they jumped all over me and hugged and kissed and asked to play this game and that and for the moment, love overflowed. Joelle and Gary and I hugged each other for a long moment, feeling the unspoken profundity of our loss. Beryl was Joelle's favorite uncle and we all loved him and missed him.

We went to dinner at a local restaurant and the next day, we would go to Aunt Mary's for a second celebration. Mary was a gem of a character, smiling, mischievous, a former head nurse who even worked in London as a nurse during World War II. After me, she was the other Italian in the Schonberger family. I looked forward to seeing her the next day. She understood; her husband had died recently and we would not have to speak a word to know what the other was feeling. However, it was now Thanksgiving night and I had to go to the Comfort Suites, by myself. I couldn't stand the idea of going into the hotel room alone. I had an idea.

I pulled Joelle over to the side and said, "How about if Joshua comes to the hotel tonight? There's an extra bed." Joelle said it was fine with her and so I asked Joshua if he'd like to come to the hotel and hang out together. He said, "Yes, I'd love it. I'll go pack my things." And so the arrangement was made. Joshua and I chatted, watched T.V., read, went to breakfast the next morning, and then drove back to pick up the gang and go to Mary's. He excitedly told his mom and dad what a great time he had.

What I didn't tell them was that Joshua, whom I met when he was 12 hours old nine years ago, saved my life that night. Joshua, the night visitor, softened the loneliness I would have endured.

"Hey, Uncle Bob, which bed should I take?"

"Take the one near the window?"

"What shall we watch on T.V.?"

"Whatever you want, Josh. Here's the remote."

"Wow, I *never* have the remote. This is great!"

The simplicity of just being together, doing simple things got me through the night. My guest needed attention and for a few moments, I could dwell on him and not on my sorrow.

When he reads this, he'll know what a godsend he was that evening. His sweet innocence pulled me through that night.

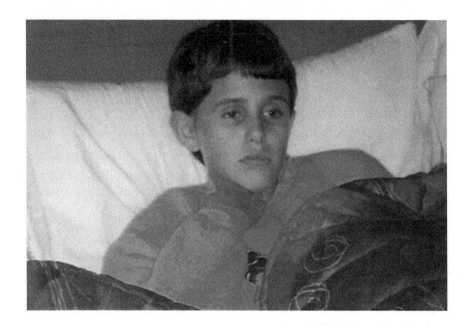

*

Three Dreams

It was the last Sunday in January 2006 when I visited the Neue Galerie on East 86th and Fifth Avenue with our friends, Beata and Don. Before leaving the museum, we walked through its Café Sabarsky, a turn of the century facsimile of a Viennese *café* equipped with period objects and artwork. It was a vibrant sunny late afternoon as some live classical music swelled in the background.

That night I had a dream.

Beryl and I were sitting at a table in the Café Sabarsky, sipping cappuccinos topped with whipped cream. We delighted in apfelstrudel, sachertorte, lekvar, and poppy seed filling pastries.

"Honey, pass me the apple strudel," I asked.

"Here, taste it, it's really good."

"Did you try the lekvar pastry? Absolutely incredible!" I declared.

"I saw that you were at the museum with Beata and Don today."

I said, "Yes, it was a beautiful exhibition pre-Hitler German art, Klimt and Schiele."

We continued with our conversation as we sipped our coffees. I was totally aware that Beryl was dead these past three months.

I then turned to him and matter-of-factly asked him, "How is it on the other side?"

I woke up startled.

A few months later, I had another dream.

I was standing on line at an H.S.B.C. A.T.M. machine on West 14th Street and Seventh Avenue, around the block from where I used to live. I recognized but couldn't quite place the deep voice that came from the person behind me. He spoke.

"I hear you're a real docta."

I turned around and it was *Beryl*. I couldn't believe it. He was kibitzing with me. I looked at him straight in the eye.

"It's *you*!"

"Yeah, it's me, honey, I thought I'd surprise you."

He was smiling broadly.

I woke up longing for him.

And still another dream. Beryl and I were at our house in the Springs, East Hampton. It was a glorious day, sunlight shining through, and he was quite buoyant. I was sitting at the counter when Beryl came from behind me and put his arms around me and uttered, "I love you."

I woke up feeling serene.

*

Some say that the dead come to visit the living. This belief presupposes an afterlife and that spirits move about and communicate freely with us. Two months after Beryl's death, a psychic told me that Beryl would be my guardian angel for the rest of my life. Talk about the year of magical thinking! However, I embraced the idea. After all, Sadie was *always* conversing with *the deads*, why couldn't I? If I could speak to them, they certainly could have a word with me.

These three dreams gave me pause. Was it my mind playing its games tapping into my unconscious desires?

Or was it something more?

I discovered the Austrian philosopher, Rudolf Steiner, taught that the dead are all around us, always there. Since the dead are with us, why not talk to them? Spirits of the dead require it, want it very much.

*

My cousin, JoAnn, first cousin to Rob and me, said she had a theory of the afterlife. The whole family is up there at a huge Italian feast and they're having a blast. At this table, there are some empty seats with name cards. Our names are on them, each of us living. The cards tell them the day we're arriving. They come over and check out the cards and say, "Oh he'll be here soon," or, "In a little while, she'll be here." They return to their gaiety and good times.

I love this fantasy. Imagine, *we'll be together again.* All of us.

Allow yourself to imagine that. *Really.*

*

Sicilians believe that there is a thin line between the living and the dead. I grew up with this belief as a matter of course. In the Scherma household, it was customary to speak about the dead as if they were living. Furthermore, they communicated with us and we with them.

Sadie claimed the dead visited her in her sleep.

"Last night, my father visited me."

"And what did he say?" I inquired.

"He told me not to worry about money. So, I won't."

My three brothers and I would ask who visited her the night before. Once she answered, "Oh, my sister Angie and Cousin Anita asked me to go dancing last night. I told them, 'Get the hell outta here.' I knew they wanted to take me over to the deads. I said, 'No way!'"

When I was younger, I had this fantasy that I would love to die dancing. When I was at a straight or gay, dance halls like The Salvation or Cheetah in the '60s or Red Parrot or The Saint in the '80s, I would just let the music infuse my body and ignite my spirit. I would dance for hours on end smiling and gliding across the dance floor. When the beat was just right, my body would move in ecstasy; I was plainly in heaven and never wanted to leave.

Accordingly, when I depart from planet earth, I want to enter a dance hall with the best of all the dance music from playlists I've heard at those clubs. Then I want to meet my guests. While I understand at death we leave our incarnations behind, that won't do for my post-death bash. I want to recognize people, as I knew them; they'll retain their best physical appearance. After all, it's *my* party.

I began to make the guest list. When somebody died, I would invite him or her to the party. Many celebrities are coming, but the most important people will be those I loved most. They will be the main attraction.

I want to see Granny, my first spiritual teacher who died when I was twenty-one. She introduced me to the notion of God as a young boy. She will still be slightly plump in a housedress with her hair in a bun wearing rimless eyeglasses. Her smile will be beaming and I will luxuriate in the tenderness of her embrace.

My seminary friends, John and Paul, who died at too young an age will be there to greet me. They were my alter egos. John was the Auntie Mame of my life who was always off to some new adventure. He was tall in stature and very Irish; he was a fine musician. Paul was the deep-feeling friend who was with me when good times went to bad. His stout Italian body and his comical spirit went together well. With each of them, it was the laughter I cherished the most. What a joyous reunion that will be!

My Aunt Angie died when I was forty. Tough and sensual like Mae West, she was buxom and blonde and had attitude. If someone was abusing another, she would step in and set them straight. She was fearless and took no prisoners. She also had the greatest laugh. When I was around her, I only had fun. I could tell her things I couldn't tell my mother; she understood life and its vicissitudes. I expect a big hug and huge smile like the day I came home from the seminary. I was home again.

My dad Frank died in 1990. I look forward to feeling the warmth of his eyes as I bask in his gentle nature. He will say again what I heard him say so long ago, "Robert, I love you and I have always loved you." He will grab my hand with both his hands and kiss me and then hug me, "Welcome home, it's been too long."

Sadie died three years later. She was always the wise one and the wise guy. I'll hold on to her for a long, long, long time.

My oldest brother, Ted, died in 1998. It was the first time a brother died. That summer I would drive to the sea, park my car, and just sit there looking out enveloped in an insurmountable sadness. He was a Brooklyn wiseass and funny as hell and he always supported my choices. He encouraged me to follow my heart, and I did. I look forward to seeing him.

My brother, Mickey, was next to go. His wife, Delia, had died 13 years prior to his death and I pledged that I would be a presence in his life for the rest of his life. Mickey taught me about the grieving process.

During the second year after Delia's death, he said, "The second year is worse than the first."

I learned that truth after Beryl died.

It was always fun to be around Mickey. He was very opinionated, very Republican, and very amusing to spend a day with. I remember he cried when he returned from Germany after a year in the army and saw me. I was a kid when he left and then I was an adolescent. We will laugh and hold onto each other.

My brother, Ron, died next after Mick. Now my three brothers were dead. A stark new reality was imposed on my life. When *Ron* died, it was just me.

Between the deaths of Mickey and Ron, the love of my life died suddenly. Three deaths in a nine-month period, that of my husband being the most shattering.

The doctors told me it was a silent heart attack that took Beryl. From that moment on, it was a broken heart that overtook me.

In marriage, we think we have ample time to get this loving thing right. Joyce Carol Oates writing about the death of her husband said, "So much to say in a marriage, so much unsaid. You assume that there will be other times, other occasions. Years."

After Beryl died, I was filled with self-recriminations. I felt that I hadn't loved adequately or strongly or well enough. Time had run out and there was nothing I could do about it. I didn't even get to say goodbye.

Assumptions make fools of us and expectations level us to the ground. I really didn't know what seems certain, is not. In the aftermath of Beryl's death,

I discovered how deeply I loved him. My longing for him taught me that. I just didn't know how much.

I want Beryl to be the first one I see when I pass. I have so much I want to say.

The End

This is thy hour, O Soul,
Thy free flight into the wordless,
Away from books, away from art,
The day erased, the lesson done,
· Thee fully forth emerging, silent
Gazing, pondering the themes thou lovest best.
Night, sleep, death, and the stars.

–Walt Whitman

Appendix

[1]

In June 1965, I completed a course in the Philosophical Foundations of Education at Brooklyn College. I was 22. Professor Maxine Greene was the instructor. In my end term paper I wrote how lost I felt that first term after I left the seminary; how tired I was of change. Professor Greene replied with a handwritten note:

Dear Mr. Scherma,

I should like to respond in kind: but doubt if I can, partly because I am aware that you see things in me that derive partly from you [which may account for the warmth and sensitivity in what you say].

The "crazy time" is the moment of crisis, which may become your moment of truth. In a sense, you are acting out one of the crucial traumas in history: the emergence from a structured, purposive universe into a universe which is as you say "huge, limitless..."

Fortunately, you welcome risk and possibility—and quest. But you are also experiencing the lost-ness which is often a function of the "new world." [Why tire of change? Why recoil from "jumping here and there?" You've chosen yourself as a seeker in an open place. [There will always be a certain tentativeness, a fundamental doubt—]

For me, this is the source of human transcendence, because only when you emerge, as you are doing, are you moved to define direction [not follow a path aid out by others], to create meaning,—to create yourself as a personality. To find a "vocation" is second to that; but your using the term, "vocation," is significant. It suggests that you will treat as a "calling" whatever work you choose to do. Remember the plan can't be wholly rational in a naughty and variable world; and it ought to be fluid; and your sense of yourself should be prior to it, not dependent on it. Oddly [or so I have found]—an awareness of one's depths [and darknessess and ambivalences] helps one choose where one ought to be moving,—even when there are no guarantees.

I don't believe that even sad times are fated to end—I believe though that the Single One can reconceive 'Sad" and "happy." —and perhaps embody them in "meaningfulness," his own, patterned design, his purpose,—which may be an embodiment, an expression of what he "truly" is.

Thank you so much.—And I wish you good seeking—, and a sense of calling soon.

Maxine Greene

My dear friend Zell is a brilliant poet and she was moved to write two poems one after my dad died in 1990 and another when my mom died in 1993.

Ciao, Father Frank

you thought the real goodbye
was a couple of years past
one of those completed processes
they pretend are real

but feel more abstract…than…
holding him, kissing him…
laughing for
Sadie's husband
silently siding with his
soap opera battle side

it's only right
he's papa

he's Frank
to the end…so sweet

letting you all prepare
with time
for his trip
out of time

a final physical embrace
brothers and all
salute to Robert's dad
Ciao, Frank, Grazie

–M. Zell Schwartzman

Sadie's Choice

Bob said, "Well, it's the end of an era."
and although I never knew them
[but for the dance in my mind's eye]
I knew he was right.

Sadie, Sadie, married lady
contessa or queen
at almost 83 decided
another season of soaps
would be a bore
her stories were fading
into a hollow yawn
her yearnings turned vividly
for sweetie, her sister,
oh, yes
her own soap was whirling/twirling
calling the grand girl
to her space—[kick high, kid!]
in the celestial Charleston

with typical toodle-doo
[so just one thing more
if it's alright with you]

Sadie finally left the house.
finally
Ciao.

—**M. Zell Schwartzman**

[4]

My godson and most loved friend, Ken, wrote a poem back in the day when we lived down the hall from each other entitled *My Godfather*:

You know I've ridden with the fear of death
And seen the devil's smile
I've felt an angel's Healing breath
Known heaven for awhile

And love, it isn't magic
Only love—but that's enough
Nothing sacred, nothing tragic
Just the elemental stuff

It holds us all together
Gives us strength to bear the pain
Let us hold onto the rainbow
At the end of every rain.

And I've loved you so profoundly
Seen your soul so crystal clear
Come with me, we'll see the sunset
And the reason why we're here.

–Ken Meissner

Acknowledgments

If God said:

"Rumi, pay homage to everything
that has helped you
enter my
arms."

there would not be one experience of my life,
not one thought, not one feeling,
nor any act, I
would not
bow
to

Spiritual Journey: Oneness Movement

Beryl was now dead two years. I recalled what my brother, Mickey, taught me after his wife, Delia, died. He said the first year was bad, but the second year was worse. I found that to be true. In the first year, the frame of reference was a year ago he was alive. A year ago, was our anniversary. A year ago, was Christmas. A year ago, was New Year's. A year ago, was my birthday. A year ago, was his birthday. A year ago, he was alive. In the second year, a year ago Beryl was dead. The shock is over; the reality sets in. In the first year, I wanted everything to be the same. In the second year, I realized nothing was the same. I was descending into an abyss, and I had to reawaken again.

I went to a workshop at Omega in Rhinebeck, New York with my friends, Michael and Leda. It was an *Awakening into Oneness* weekend seminar. The woman running it was an Indian dasa, a guide and adherent of the oneness movement. I was not much interested in a movement; I had already done the Catholic Church and did not want to replace one set of rules and beliefs with another. What I was interested in was the Oneness blessing, *deeksha*. People who became blessing-givers transmitted a hands-on energy to the head. This positive force reportedly completes trauma and heals relationship. Sometimes one's perspective changes suddenly and dramatically. Sometimes it imparts peace in the recipient. Our experience of separation disappears and we experience oneness with the universe.

August, 2008, Deeksha In Fiji

That weekend at Omega had a multi-layered effect on me. I joined a Oneness monthly group that met on the Upper West Side. After a brief teaching, I received *deeksha* from several blessing-givers each meeting and went into a contemplative state. These people were joyous, peaceful, loving. It was a good spiritual space with no fear and abundant peace. I knew I wanted to take the next step.

I decided to become a blessing-giver. The training was in Fiji. I went alone. Arriving at Kennedy late at night and I met a woman named Sandy. She was going to the training as well. We became buddies.

The week-long instruction started each day with yoga, then meditation, then breakfast, then seminar learning, then lunch, more training, then dinner, then meditation again. It was vegetarian fare. In fact, they recommended no alcohol two months prior to arriving in Fiji. I did that effortlessly. I was ready for the next step, wherever that took me.

The camaraderie and reflective atmosphere was reminiscent of my seminary days. Laughing, enjoying meals together, meditating in silence, communing with the still voice within was exactly what I wanted.

Sandy came to Fiji to heal her relationship with her father. She moved him into her home and was caring for him.

Mary came to heal her relationship with her son.

Jim was trying to figure out the next part of his life. He was in his early fifties and not ready for retirement. He simply wanted some clarity as he moved forward.

Two college-aged sisters wanted to explore what choices they would have after school.

A couple from Australia wanted to expand their relationship so they could be of more service to others.

An executive from Fox International Studios was providing schooling and guidance for impoverished kids in Thailand. He had given up his lucrative career to be of service. He wanted to bring the healing power of *deeksha* to that venue.

One woman was very private but most certainly had a personal intention she wanted to fulfill.

The *dasa* assigned to my group was Sujay. He asked me why I came to Fiji. I told him I was trying to get past Beryl's death. He acknowledged that I was in pain.

I said, "Pain is my daily companion."

Sujay then drew a distinction between pain and suffering.

"The pain you're experiencing is intense and I suggest that you submit to it when it comes up. Your psyche will handle only as much as it can and then shut down."

I knew that was true. I was committed to feeling every possible response to Beryl's death.

"Now, suffering is different. Where pain is involuntary, suffering is a choice."

"I don't understand."

He explained that pain is an experience we have; suffering is how we relate to that experience. Remaining present with the experience of pain can be healing and transformative. But suffering can cause you to get lost in the pain and can make you feel hopeless because there is no release from the pain. Suffering is the story we make up about the pain we're experiencing.

"So, if I am in pain about not telling Beryl all things I thought necessary before he died, I can endlessly hate myself for not doing that."

"Right."

"And I can decide on the spot to dismiss that thought and replace it with something like, 'Beryl knew I loved him and I knew he loved me.'"

Sujay agreed emphatically and said I didn't have to indulge in suffering about what could have been, what should have been, or what would have been.

"The loss of someone you love is painful enough. You don't need to add recriminations and suffer. The trick is to catch yourself in the act of suffering."

By the end of the week, the three *dasas* introduced us to an enlightened being who was in a state of ecstatic bliss. He was out of his mind, literally. Laughing hysterically, he placed his hands on each of our heads and by so doing, we became *deeksha*-givers. We could now give *deeksha* either by hands-on transmission or simply by intention. There was much joy in the room and now it was time to party!

The music blared on, dancing was the imperative, and lots of laughter and joy. One *dasa* shouted out.

"Give everybody *deeksha*!"

Then, "Give your ancestors *deeksha*!"

Then, "Give objects *deeksha*!"

Then, "If people don't want *deeksha*, give it to them anyway."

The next night we had a feast and even some wine and meat.

When I got home, the first person I gave *deeksha* to was my nephew and godson, Tom. I gave him ear pods attached to my iPod and played some soothing Indian chant. I blessed him by placing my hands on his forehead, then the top of his head, and then the back. He stayed quietly in the moment of *deeksha* enhanced by the melody he was listening. After a few minutes, he said he felt something. Something peaceful. I think what gets transmitted is simply the energy of love. My love for Tom, whom I knew for all of his forty-four years, went through my hands. I think the power of love connects with the Love that is between us all, a commanding force.

I have a basket where I have placed the names of all those I want to give *deeksha*. I do so when I pass that basket.

I give *deeksha* to the *living*, my friends.

I bless my dear friend, Zell, who was my teacher for *A Course in Miracles*, who is a miracle herself. Her sharp intelligence and wit, her willingness to listen, her ability to give me encouragement and support, got me through some of the darkest nights after Beryl died.

I bless Beryl and Gail who were ever present after Beryl's death. Beryl called me every single morning for over a year to make sure I was okay. Gail insisted on knowing where I was when I wasn't in her sight. Later on, I got legal credentials to officiate weddings and I married these two women. In the meantime, we traveled to Venice, Florence, London, Paris, Amsterdam,

Dublin, Australia, and San Miguel, Mexico. My heart overflows with my love for them.

I bless their adult children, Dara, a talented dancer, and Bradley married to Lauren and their kids Emily, Rebecca, and Zach and their dog, Luke.

I bless Arthur and Anthony who loved Beryl so.

I bless Michael and Leda, my fellow travelers, who came to the house in East Hampton the *first* weekend I went there after Beryl died. Their love and caring sustained me that whole weekend. Our love for each other continues. I have such fun with them.

I bless their son, Eric, always who is a vulnerable, sensitive, highly intelligent being as he finds his way in the world. I have always had a special connection to him since he was a child. He is a fellow seeker who knows the meaning of pain and because of that he is also very, very funny!

I bless Eric's brother, Griffin, who is a healer currently training in Chinese herbal medicine and acupuncture. Griff has the capacity to really have a good time, no matter where he is. I bless his future wife, Neaz.

I bless Beata and now deceased Don who simply continued as usual after Beryl's death: a dinner date, a movie, a museum. I cherish our warm friendship.

I bless Babs and Al who did the same and made sure to be a presence in my life. Their warmth is always a comfort to me.

I bless Dawn, my loving friend and neighbor, for the gift she is to me, the gift that keeps on giving. Her generous spirit has no bounds.

I bless Richard, my Jamaican son and ex-student who is now my friend. He insists he's *still* twenty-five years old. We always keep in touch. He's now working in Nairobi, Kenya.

I bless Carole, Liz, Howie, and Eileen, my Columbus High School buddies who called me, went to the theater, invited me to events, and just made life without Beryl tolerable, even fun.

I bless Maureen, Cynthia (and her husband Mike), Jerry, and Bette-Lee who formed great friendships at Cahner's Publishing and became my friends. Bette-Lee became my punctuation maven!

I bless Bea and Sandy (and her husband Bill) and Buddy and the late Diane P., members of the Birthday Club. So much fun all these years. Still.

I bless Melissa, my memoir teacher and coach and one of my favorite writers. She loved Sadie and Beryl on the page and encouraged me to write on. Her commentaries were *most* helpful. I just love her. Always will.

I bless my memoir classmates for the safe space they created for two and a half years as we wrote about the most poignant and defenseless times of our lives.

I bless Erica, my dear friend and mentor, a talented writer who edited my writing all these years. We are a mutual admiration society; we love each other's writing and we simply love each other all these years since 1970. We are "Old Friends."

I bless Andrew and his sister, Kathy both of whom I love without limit.

I bless Ken, whom I've known since sophomore year in high school. He has been a source of intelligent comfort and lots of laughs to this very day.

I give *deeksha* to the *living,* my family.

I bless Gloria who simply was present, especially in conversation. We have been talking since we know each other since I was a kid and she a teenager. She shared her grieving over my brother, Ted, that facilitated and shed light on mine.

I bless her children Frank, Tom, Doug, and Krystyne for their phone calls, their barbecues, and their holiday parties. A kind word from one of them or a kind gesture meant the world to me at a given moment.

I bless their spouses and all my great nieces and great nephews and now a great, great niece and another on the way.

I bless my niece and godchild, Karen, who understood the enormity of losing Beryl and my three brothers, one of them her father, by simply saying so.

I bless her sister, Lisa, who, in her own way, let me know her caring.

I bless my niece and godchild, Stacey, whose father, my brother, Ron, died a few months after Beryl. That shared pain will last a lifetime.

I bless Alex, Ron, and Dorie's son, who has become closer to me over the years. He's now doing stand-up comedy.

I bless all my great nieces and nephews: Nick, Alec, Jenna, Kristoff, Raymond, Grayson, Gianna, Lucca, Sabrina, Patrick, Delia, and Joey.

I bless Joelle and Gary and Joshua, and the twins Jescey and Jadyn and Jarek and Jenaye in Allentown, whom I treasure even after all these years after Beryl's death. There are no words that can capture our abundant love for each other.

I bless Mary Schonberger, Beryl's Italian aunt, who has always been in my corner with laughter and more laughter. Mary, very Catholic, always tells me that she's praying to God for a new *friend* for me.

I bless Beryl's sister, Sarilyn and Steve, her husband. Still a strong and loving presence in my life.

I bless Beryl's brother, Gerry, and his wife, Sue, who are always fun.

I bless Beryl's younger sibling, Arne, who always refers to me as *brother*, and his wife, Connie. I bless Arne's sons, Lyle and David, who has become a classical trombone virtuoso.

I bless my cousin, JoAnn, whose wise-cracking, lower East Side demeanor has always been refreshing. As we age, we're getting closer and closer.

I bless my cousin, Robert, whom I consider a brother, for his caring, for his listening, for his capacity to laugh, and make me laugh. He is the funniest person I know! He means more to me than he knows.

Sometimes, I have a falling out with friends. I get furious and call them assholes, but that's just ego. In the next moment, I come from Spirit and give them *deeksha*.

My higher self wins the day, even though I'm still furious.

I give deeksha to the *dead*.

I bless Beryl.

I bless my mom, Sadie.

I bless my dad, Frank.

I bless my brother Ted.

I bless my brother Mickey.

I bless my brother Ron.

I bless Aunt Jo, who died at almost 104, who cooked Christmas dinner for us when she was 102 and 103!

I bless my Uncle Vince, Aunt Jo's husband.

I bless Granny and Pop, *and* my dad's parents whom I never met.

I bless all my ancestors.

I bless Mick's wife, Delia, and Ron's first wife, Jean.

I bless Beryl's parents, Dorothy, and Joe.

I bless my beloved Aunt Angie and Uncle Ray.

I bless my seminary buddies, Paul Petrillo and John Manning.

I bless my friend and Fort Hamilton High colleague, Jim. We laughed so much.

I believe that anyone can give *deeksha*. Anyone. It's no special power or skill. It's a matter of intention. One of my fellow memoir writers, Jessica, always gave me *deeksha* because I told her she could. Jessica died recently and I know she's giving me *deeksha* at this very moment. I loved her so. Still do. In memoir class, she told me that when Sadie appeared on the page, she lit it up. Makes me smile.

Behind all this, some great happiness is hiding.

–Yehuda Amichai

CPSIA information can be obtained
at www.ICGtesting.com
Printed in the USA
BVHW052308100921
616517BV00002B/110